The City and the Saloon

The Cow and the Saloon

University Press of Colorado

© 1996 by the University Press of Colorado
© 1982 by the University of Nebraska Press
Published by the University Press of Colorado
P.O. Box 849
Niwot, Colorado 80544
(303) 530-5337

The University Press of Colorado is a cooperative publishing enterprise supported, in part, by Adams State College, Colorado State University, Fort Lewis College, Mesa State College, Metropolitan State College of Denver, University of Colorado, University of Northern Colorado, University of Southern Colorado, and Western State College of Colorado.

The paper used in this publication meets the minimum requirements of the national Standard for Information Sciences—Permanence of Paper for Printed Library Materials. ANSI Z39.48—1984

Library of Congress Cataloging in Publication Data

Noel, Thomas J. (Thomas Jacob)
      The city and the saloon : Denver, 1858-1916 / by Thomas J. Noel
        p. cm.
      Originally published : Lincoln : University of Nebraska Press, c1982. With new introd.
      Includes bibliographical references (p.   ) and index.
      ISBN 0-87081-426-5 (paper : alk. paper)
      1. Bars (Drinking establishments)--Colorado--Denver--History.
  2. Denver (Colo.)--History. 3. Denver (Colo.)--Social life and customs. I. Title
GT3811.D46N63 1996
647.95788 ' 83--dc20   96-30218
                                                      CIP

to
Margaret Jacob

Contents

Tables

Maps

Illustrations

Preface to the 1996 Reprint

Saloons are changing. Their numbers and hours of operation have been reduced by recent court rulings on liability laws that hold bartenders and bar owners responsible for the actions of their customers. Since 1985, Duffy's Shamrock Tavern even closes on St. Patrick's Day to duck lawsuits from litigious inebriates. Denver's oldest tavern, opened as the Christopher Columbus Hall in the 1870s, closed in 1995 after numerous drugs arrests.

The dominant culture, of course, has long used drug laws to control subgroups and close their haunts—be they the Irish, Italians, and Germans targeted by Prohibitionists, or the Chinese who could be arrested after opium was outlawed, or the Hispanics and Indians using drugs of their choice.

Bars have evolved into more sober establishments in our neopuritanical age. Alcohol is in greater disrepute than at any time since Prohibition. Bars are once again being stereotyped as the havens of the irresponsible, the sexually promiscuous, criminals, drug dealers, drunk drivers, and—gasp—smokers!

The old-time saloon, as this book attempts to document in detail, could be sorted out ethnically by the country of origin of the owner and/or employees. Most ethnic bars have disappeared, with the exception of Hispanic bars, which often remain Spanish-speaking havens of that culture.

Taverns that once could be sorted out by ethnic group now seem easier to catalog by the age or sexual preference of the customers (geriatric bars and yuppie bars, singles bars and gay bars). The gay community has emerged in recent decades from a barroom culture similar to that of the ethnic saloons that nourished nineteenth-century immigrant groups. Not only socializing but much of the organizing, politicizing, and AIDS awareness and prevention revolves around the city's gay bars. Gays find the saloon a protective and nourishing organization, where group behavior is sanctioned and the disapproving general public is discouraged from participation.

One type of saloon has not only survived but flourished—the "sports bar." Televised athletic contests draw bargoers galore. In Denver a dozen new sports bars sprouted up in the shadow of Coors Field in 1995 when this baseball park opened as the home of the Colorado Rockies. Of course in the old days "sporting" men were noted for gambling and "sporting" girls for prostitution. The term *sporting* did not become respectable until after the national cleansing of Prohibition.

Most of the saloons mentioned here are long gone. A notable exception is the Buckhorn Exchange, now both a National Register and Denver landmark. Taverns are generally not regarded as fit for preservation, certainly not in a league with churches and schoolhouses. Elderly bars are commonly knocked down and perhaps replaced with new chain restaurant bars (Bennigans, Chili's, Hooters, Houlihan's, TGI Fridays, and so on), which mimic old-time saloons. These sanitized re-creations are distant mirrors of the dim, folklore-shrouded taverns examined in the following pages.

Acknowledgments

At Aunt Margaret's one night, Dale Reed and I came up with the idea. Why not do a systematic, documented survey of every bar in Denver? We thought this would be a novel approach to the social, political, and economic life of the city. It was already ten o'clock on Friday night, March 24, 1972, and the idea almost drowned us in euphoria. Aunt Margaret came out of her bedroom, followed by her cat with the question mark tail.

"What are you two raving about?" We told her and she was appalled. "Haven't you anything better to do?"

That night we visited the first three of some six hundred bars in the City and County of Denver. Over the next couple of years, with the companionship and research assistance of a great many people, I visited practically every bar in town, collecting lore and historical and demographic information on each. This survey provided an introduction to my study of Denver's rapidly disappearing preprohibition saloon buildings.

In one of the old wooden booths at the Frontier Hotel Bar (now the site of the Denver Center for the Performing Arts), Lyle W. Dorsett, my mentor at the University of Colorado at Denver, suggested ways in which the saloon could be used as a window on urban history. Subsequently, the project became my doctoral dissertation at the University of Colorado at Boulder. Professors Robert G. Athearn, Matt Downey, Ralph Mann, and Bill Taylor guided me through longer, more sober years of research, analysis, and rewriting. Elliott West, whose *The Saloon on the Rocky Mountain Mining Frontier* and other writings helped to guide my work, also offered encouragement, suggestions, and a most helpful manuscript review.

The employees of the Colorado Historical Society library, Western History Department of the Denver Public Library, Federal Records Center in Denver, Western Historical Collections at Norlin Library in Boulder, Bancroft Library in Berkeley, Huntington Library in San Marino, Newberry Library in Chicago, and Baker Business Library at Harvard all offered their expertise and access to their collections. The courts, county clerk, election commission, planning office, and police department of the City and County of Denver allowed me to rummage through their records. The Colorado State Supreme Court Library, Colorado State Archives, and Colorado Health Department's Bureau of Vital Statistics granted access to their records.

Louisa Ward Arps, Lyle Dorsett, Jay Fell, Mark Foster, Dave Halaas, Jim Kedro, Steve Leonard, the late Terry Mangan, Bette Peters, Dale Reed, Jim Wright, and others reviewed all or part of the manuscript, making corrections and suggestions. Richard Edwards not only joined many of the tavern and library research expeditions but drew the maps, helped to computerize some of the data, and served as a research assistant. Research papers of my students at the University of Colorado at Denver, the University of Denver, and Metropolitan State College uncovered new sources and angles that supplemented my own. I am also grateful to countless bartenders, barmaids, bar owners, and barstool commentators.

Cecilia Burkhardt, Dennis Gallagher, Glee Georgia, Ada Mangini Joy, the late Terry Mangan, Augie Mastrogiuseppe, Sam Morrison, Bette Peters, Diane Rabson, Roger Whitacre, Charles Woolley, and Jim Wright generously presented photographs and information. The National Science Foundation provided funds for research travel, computer time, and a research assistant.

My wife Vi helped with research and writing and supported me in many other ways during this decade-long project. Instead of a more conventional courtship, she cheerfully helped with the survey of Denver's lowest dives.

Aunt Margaret, who was skeptical about this project from the beginning, read and reread the manuscript in many stages, always finding new errors and fuzzy thinking to eliminate. She always had corrections, suggestions, and hot coffee waiting in the morning.

The City and the Saloon

Chapter 1
CONFLUENCE

The Rocky Mountains, when they saw them at last, thrilled both husband and wife. Together they urged on the oxen. Twenty-four-year-old Lavinia Porter later confided to her diary:

> As we came closer to Denver the South Platte seemed to make its nearest approach to beauty, and in many places was studded with beautiful islands, picturesque indeed with their emerald green foliage of graceful willows. . . . I remember how joyfully we greeted the first scrubby pine trees, giving us hope that the desert was nearly past and the mountains not far off. Their soft and tender green was soothing to our sun-burnt vision.[1]

With thousands of others, the Porters headed for the confluence of the South Platte River and Cherry Creek, birthplace of the Colorado gold rush. Lavinia marveled at the stream of humanity stretching some seven hundred miles from the Missouri River frontier towns to the gold diggings. By day the emigrant procession stirred up an endless column of dust and by night campfires flickered along the Platte as far as the eye could see.

Lavinia thought these argonauts a motley lot: sunburnt men with long, shaggy hair and women in sunbonnets wearing tattered dresses shortened by campfires. Some of these migrants had been relieved to cross the Missouri and see the old, familiar institutions fall behind. Others, including Lavinia, grew apprehensive as they passed the last church, the last school, the last county courthouse, and the last jail.

Only saloons seemed to be moving west as fast as the people. On the Platte River road between Omaha and Denver, dozens of roadhouses had sprung up by 1860. They were often the first and sometimes the only public building in new frontier settlements. These saloons bore little resemblance to traditional eastern inns. Rather, they were unique to the frontier—a crudely

1

improvised combination of a grocery and a dry goods store that seemed to specialize in wet goods.

Cottonwood trees, called "sweet cottonwoods" in the barren West, served as the first wayside inns. Under their broad-leafed boughs, the pioneers camped, socialized, and drank. And when the time came to build taverns, these trees became walls and tables and chairs. Small branches and bark were used to chink the inside and mud was plastered on the outside. Split saplings were draped over the ridgepole and sod piled on to complete the roof. When moisture fell on these dirt roofs, muddy water dripped for days indoors after the rain had stopped. In the spring, the mud roofs bloomed with wildflowers.

Other early saloons came west on wheels, whiskey-filled wagons converted to grogshops and painted with advertisements such as "Old Bourbon Whiskey sold here." Still other entrepreneurs made tent taverns of their canvas wagon tops, while the more ambitious knocked down their wagons to make shack saloons with canvas roofs.

Travelers who scorned these early inns might stop at farms or ranches at dinnertime, hoping for a kitchen-cooked meal and a bed for the night. Lonesome frontier families generally welcomed these "sundowners." But one Platte Valley rancher, tired of questions, requests, and sundowning, hung on his gate a human skull inscribed "Died from asking too many questions."[2] Others beseiged by the argonaut army converted their homes to roadhouses, where travelers could eat, drink, and sleep for a price. Colonel John D. Henderson, whose ranch lay a dozen miles downriver from Denver, announced in an 1859 issue of the *Rocky Mountain News* the opening of Henderson House. Other South Platte pioneers, including D'Aubrey, Sanders, and Pierson, also converted their ranches to roadhouses.

These protosaloons and their "tangle-foot," "shake-knee," "rot-gut," and "bust-head" whiskeys were memorably repulsive for genteel travelers such as Lavinia Porter and the French mining engineer Louis Simonin. Washing facilities were often dirtier than their customers. When folks sought the outhouse, they were in for an adventure. Not only insects but rodents, reptiles, and skunks thrived behind the crescent moon doors. Colorado waystations of the 1860s, as Simonin wrote to his family in France, had a basin of water, soap, "and a towel that turns without end around a roller." He also found "mirrors, combs, brushes of all kinds, even toothbrushes, fastened by a long string, so that everyone may help himself and no one carry it off. You would laugh in Paris at these democratic customs; here they are accepted by all and even welcomed, unless perhaps the toothbrush, which is regarded with a suspicious eye."[3]

These primitive bars did offer shade, shelter, a warm stove, and news of what lay ahead. The tavernkeeper was a frontier source of news, gossip, and advice. Some innkeepers had even met members of William Green Russell's party from Georgia which had first found "color" in the Platte during the summer of 1858. Although no other significant discovery came that year, trailside tavernkeepers reassured gold seekers that early in 1859 George A. Jackson and John H. Gregory had located gold in Clear Creek. By 1860, some forty thousand argonauts funneled into Colorado along the South Platte and Arkansas trails.

Where these routes converged at the confluence of the Platte and Cherry Creek, town boomers and merchants established the rival towns of Auraria and Denver City in the fall of 1858. Among the stream of emigrants arriving in the twin settlements in the spring of 1860 were the Porters. Colorado's green foothills, jubilant streams, and snow-capped peaks led Lavinia to forget the vow, recorded in her diary, that she and her husband had made back east: "We had decided and promised each other that if Pike's Peak and its environments did not come up to our expectations that we would push on to California."

In Denver, emigrants camped along the river and swapped stories with travelers who had taken the Smoky Hill and Arkansas River routes. These pilgrims also spoke of a string of roadhouses along their trail. Twenty miles southeast of Denver, where the southern branch of the Smoky Hill Trail struck Cherry Creek, stood the Twenty Mile House. An English traveler reported that the proprietor, Nelson Dowd, was a cheerful Irishman who tended bar while his wife and daughters looked after the cooking. Guests might intimidate the Irishman, but not his wife. When a ruffian known as Tiger Bill became obstreperous, "there came a flash of petticoats, and Mrs. Dowd, who had been listening from behind the door to the kitchen, darted into the bar with a feminine screech and set her ten commandments in his face, dragging her nails down each cheek."[4] Perhaps because of such unruly customers, the Dowds sold their waystation to James J. Parker, who gave his name to the town that grew up around the now gone Twenty Mile House.

Seventeen, Twelve, Nine, Seven, and Four Mile Houses also greeted those following Cherry Creek to its confluence with the Platte. Seventeen Mile House still rests in the shade of a tremendous cottonwood tree that, if legend is true, hides the grave of someone murdered in the roadhouse. Warned that the sheriff was coming, the murderer hastily buried the corpse and planted the tree to disguise the grave.

Twelve Mile House tavernkeeper Johnnie Melvin kept his post office in the barroom so that he could attend to both at one time. Twelve Mile House, or Melvin House, featured dinner dances with fiddlers brought out from Denver. For the trip into town, stage drivers of the 1860s often borrowed Melvin's fine white race horses to replace their mangy, travel-worn mules so that well-heeled passengers could arrive in Denver with éclat.

The California miners who built Four Mile House sold it in 1860 to a jolly widow, Mary Cawker. Mary continued to run it as an inn, but she and her daughter supposedly used the upstairs as a dance hall. After the dances, guests pulled out muslin room dividers on strings and bedded down in buffalo robes on the pine floor. In the morning, the Cawkers served coffee, fries, beans, and salty meat downstairs in the tavern where guests could linger for a drink and a view of the gold-laced Rockies. "A neat little tavern," one traveler called the cottonwood-shaded waystation in 1866, with "very sweet and cold" well water as well as stronger libations. Over a century later, this pioneer roadhouse on the Cherry Creek route to Denver has been restored and is now a museum and historic park.[5]

If taverns bordered the trails into the gold-rush crossroads, Denver itself was infested with saloons, according to Lavinia Porter's diary. She found

> An exceedingly primitive town consisting of numerous tents and numbers of rude and illy constructed cabins, with nearly as many rum shops and low saloons as cabins. . . . Many of the squalid adventurers lived in the crudest manner with no law save the Vigilance Committee. No wonder that so many coming into this dismal village, chafed and irritated with the long journey, were disheartened and discouraged and turned their faces homeward.

After a few disagreeable days in Denver, the Porters sold their wedding crystal to one of the fancier saloons for sorely needed cash and set out northward along the Cherokee Trail to Fort Laramie and the path to California.

Many of the early-day saloons clustered along Ferry Street (present-day Eleventh Street) for the same reason that other businesses congregated there—at the end of the street (which waded into the South Platte) was Thomas Warren's ferry, a crude raft hauled by ropes. The ferry created the first bottleneck for the thousands of people funneling through Denver to the mountains. Capitalizing on the presence of the jammed-up gold rushers, merchants of wet and dry goods set up shop along the dirt path called Ferry Street (see map 1).

At least one early inn opened there in 1859 because a couple could not afford Warren's one-dollar ferry fee. "We had started for Pikes Peak," Mrs. Samuel Dolman reminisced later

> but had run out of money could not pay our fare accross the Platt river on a improvised pine log boat we had taken plenty of provisions and a no. 7 charter oak stove I commenced baking bread, pies and cookies sold them out readily for thare was so many men that had done thare own cooking they wanted a change I got good prices for my cooking. . . . We soon had a house up boarded up and down liek you would build a barn the windows was covered with canvas it was the first house inclosed with lumber. . . . we took plank and made tables and bedsteads and benches to sit on. . . . it was called the Kansas House.[6]

4

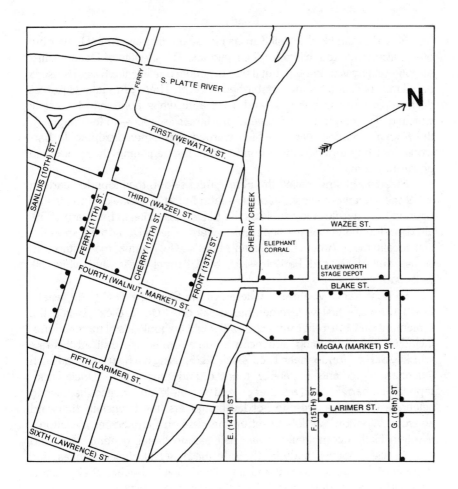

Map 1. Denver Saloons in 1860

Mrs. Dolman liked to call Kansas House the first tavern in Denver but others also made that claim for their saloons. The identity of Denver's first saloon building is unknown, but it was probably one like the River House, a bar, dance hall, and brothel established in 1859. Three years later vigilantes declared it a public nuisance and set it afire while approving townsfolk watched. The bartender and several prostitutes escaped—to the chagrin of the *Rocky Mountain News,* which warned that other disreputable bars would also be burned to the ground.[7] From the beginning, the saloon had powerful enemies.

Rice and Heffner called the Ferry Street saloon they founded early in 1859 the settlement's first. "Count" Henri Murat and David Smoke, who opened their dirt-floor log cabin as the El Dorado Hotel in February 1859, also boasted that it was the first public tavern. The El Dorado did sport the first, locally made American flag after Murat's wife, Katrina, made stars and stripes out of her red Parisian skirt, blue flannel dress, and white silk petticoat.[8]

Richens Lacy Wootton, a veteran of the Santa Fe Trail trade, established Denver's first well-remembered saloon. "Uncle Dick" visited the settlement on Christmas Eve, 1858, with eight wagonloads of merchandise, including Taos Lightning. American mountain men had distilled this raw whiskey at Rio Hondo, near Taos, since 1825, using a wheat base and such legendary ingredients as pepper, tobacco, and gunpowder. "Uncle Dick" tapped one barrel, stood another on end as a table, and invited the town to celebrate Christmas. Despite holiday hangovers, the townsfolk afterward awarded Wootton free lots to set up business on Ferry Street. Wootton's Western Hall, a combination town hall, saloon, hotel, general store, and ten-pin alley, opened early in 1859. In the new city of clay, canvas, and cottonwood, Wootton's story-and-a-half hewn log hall with its shake shingle roof and glass windows was judged the grandest structure.

"Uncle Dick's" remained a center of activity until he left town in 1862. "I reckon I shouldn't have felt right," the old mountain man explained later, "after the buildings got too thick. There would have been a lack of room and breathing space and I might have been expected to wear fine clothes."[9] Notwithstanding this Virginia-born westerner's professed desire for elbow room, he was probably forced out of town for his sympathies with the Confederacy.

After Wootton opened his Ferry Street hall, other taverners located nearby. Thomas Pollock, the first elected sheriff and hangman, augmented his salary (fifty cents for each person he jailed) by opening Pollock House. As the first two-story building in the Cherry Creek area, Pollock's frame boarding house and tavern towered several feet over Wootton's hall and all other competitors. William A. McFadding, a member of the Russell party from Georgia that first discovered gold in the vicinity and first president of the Auraria Town Company, opened another Ferry Street tavern. By 1860,

Auraria's main street strip included John H. Ming's International Billiard Hall, sporting six slate and marble tables; Ed Karczewsky and Henry Reitz's bakery and lager beer saloon; Jefferson House; Vasquez House; Jack O'Neill's Capitol Saloon; and James Reid's Hall, offering music and minstrel shows.[10]

Saloon-crowded Ferry Street thrived and Auraria initially grew faster than Denver City across the creek. To help convince newcomers of the superior merits of Auraria, John Smith, the mountain man and treasurer of the Auraria Town Company, kept a free-flowing keg in his cabin. Smith's friend George Bent, the mixed-blood son of fort keeper William Bent, observed that "every new arrival, and especially the storekeepers, had to be fought over, each town-company offering inducements and squabbling over the relative advantages of their two 'cities.' When Auraria secured a new merchant there was gloom in Denver, and when Denver succeeded in capturing another grocer there was gnashing of teeth in Auraria."[11]

At first, Denver looked like Auraria's parking lot. Newcomers tied down their wagons and left their livestock in Denver City's various corrals, of which the Elephant Corral was the largest. The Elephant, which opened in the spring of 1858, occupied much of the block between Fourteenth, Wazee, Fifteenth, and Blake Streets. It was named, in the talk of the 1850s, for those coming to "see the elephant," to see what the excitement in the golden West was all about. At the Elephant, emigrants watered and fed their livestock, traded their prairie oxen for mountain mules, and bought, sold, and rented four-footed transportation.

After stabling their animals in the corral, owners flocked to the adjacent Denver House, a combination saloon, hotel, and gambling "hell." Notorious for bad whiskey and crooked gamblers, the Denver House proved hazardous to unsuspecting newcomers from the states. Some of these pilgrims spent their first night in Denver celebrating at the bar, then moved to the gaming tables, and finally fell asleep or passed out on the dirt floor.

Waking up broke and hung over in the morning sunshine, Denver House initiates could survey the long, low structure, 130 feet by 36 feet, with a bar that ran the entire length of the building. On shelves behind the bar sat bottles of murky liquid with pretentious labels. A rain barrel in the corridor provided the only water—once guests brushed aside the scum and insects. Across the corridor lay the first-class bedrooms, six small canvas cubicles with cottonwood stump chairs. The Denver House and Elephant Corral complex was "the center of civilization," according to the gambler Edward Chase, where "they roped 'em in"—both livestock and greenhorns.[12]

The Elephant's importance diminished after the arrival of a new transportation network. General William H. Larimer, Jr. the fifty-year-old town promoter who established Denver City on a claim he had jumped, had schemed even before he left Leavenworth to get a stagecoach connection. As a latecomer and an underdog in rivalry with the larger Auraria Town

7

Company, the organization established by the Russell party from Georgia, Larimer had to gamble. His Denver City Town Company gave fifty-three lots to the Russell, Majors and Waddell express company, six lots to the firm's president, William H. Russell (unrelated to the Russells from Georgia), and a strategic two-lot site at Fifteenth and Blake streets for the outfit's Denver office. After the Leavenworth and Pike's Peak stages began rumbling into Denver in May of 1859, Auraria, as George Bent put it, "turned up its toes and died."[13]

In the spring of 1860, at a midnight ceremony on the Larimer Street bridge, the settlements were consolidated. Denver was the name given to the new city. Once dominant Auraria became simply West Denver.

Within the consolidated city, merchants began maneuvering to get as close as possible to the stage depot at Fifteenth and Blake streets. A new urban nucleus sprang up there, replacing the original one on Ferry Street. The post office moved from Auraria's Vasquez House to the Denver side of Cherry Creek. The *Rocky Mountain News,* whose first office had been in the attic of Wootton's Hall, moved to a neutral site in the creek bed. After the *News* was washed off its stilts by the flood of 1864, editor William N. Byers also moved to the Denver side.

Seeking the new center of commercial gravity, dozens of saloonkeepers opened bars near the stage depot to tempt dusty, tired, and thirsty travelers with ice-cold beer and warm whiskey. Ed Chase opened his first Denver gambling saloon a few doors down from the depot on Blake Street. Chase's mulatto friend, Barney Ford, a runaway slave, launched his drinking, eating, sleeping, and tonsorial parlor across the street from the depot. Missouri House and Jefferson House migrated from Auraria to bustling Blake Street.

Blake enjoyed main-street status for only a couple of years. Ben Holladay purchased the stage line in 1862 and moved its terminal a year or two later to a two-story brick building at Fifteenth and Market streets, the first story of which still stands. After the stage office moved, Market and Larimer Streets became a center of commercial activity. By 1867 the *News* described Blake Street as an "ancient thoroughfare" where only "two or three eating and beer saloons, and two upstairs billiard saloons comprise the evening business."[14] As retail business left, Blake became the wholesale, warehouse, and flophouse district. Thus began the decline of lower downtown Denver, a trend not reversed until a century later.

The shifting numbers and locations of saloons reflected these changes in the city's commerce. In 1860, twelve of the town's thirty-five saloons rimmed Ferry Street, while only eight bordered Blake Street. By 1866, however, the first Denver business directory listed only four saloons and boarding houses on Ferry and a dozen on Blake. A decade later, Larimer and Market had emerged as the principal saloon streets.

During the territorial period (1858–76), the great majority of some 270 Denver saloons operated within a twelve-block area surrounding the stage depots. Over one-third (96) of them were on Blake, 59 were on Larimer and 38 were on Market. Although some saloons moved into the suburbs along railroad and streetcar lines after 1870, liquor houses remained largely confined to the core city until prohibition in 1916.

In the years to come, as the city expanded beyond the frontier nucleus and developed neighborhoods where bars were unwelcome, saloons became more or less permanent fixtures on many downtown street corners, although their names and proprietors changed over the years (cf. map 1 with maps 4 and 7). With the restoration of lower downtown that began in the 1960s, taverns returned to some of the surviving structures that had housed nineteenth-century saloons. In this ever changing city, the concentration of saloons at the core has been constant.

The replacement of wood, mud, and clay "shebangs" with brick can be traced to April 19, 1863, when early-morning revelers were carousing in the Cherokee House, a frame doggery. Perhaps a tipsy drinker knocked over an oil lamp or a candle; at any rate, the back room burst into flame. Winds fanned the fire and by sunrise the business district was a blackened waste.

Denver businessmen quickly rebuilt, using inexpensive pinkish bricks made from local clay. Where Cherokee House had stood catercorner to the Leavenworth stage depot, Henry Fuerstein opened the Occidental Billiard Hall and Reading Rooms in an attractive two-story brick structure. Barney Ford borrowed nine thousand dollars from the Kountze Brothers' Colorado National Bank to rebuild with brick on his old site. Instead of his one-story shack, Ford now had a basement barber shop, first-floor restaurant and second-story saloon hall. Gus Fogus built next door on Blake Street, opening the handsome beer garden he called Atlantic Hall. Gambler Ed Chase also rebuilt, erecting his elaborate Palace next to the ashes of the Denver House and Elephant Corral.

Borrowing an idea from the Mexicans already settled in Colorado, some pioneers built of mud and straw bricks, or "dobies." Adobe proved quite satisfactory until the Denver building code banned it. Mayor William J. Barker approved an ordinance in the 1870s restricting the size of bricks to 8¼ by 4 1/16 by 2¼ inches and precluding the use of adobe bricks, which are considerably larger. A later ordinance further required that bricks be dried in ovens and not in the sun.[15] With perhaps unconscious, but nevertheless effective, discrimination, settlers from the states kept adobe-dwelling Mexicans from feeling at home.

Along Blake, Market and Larimer streets, the red-brick rows of boarding house saloons became home for many of the gold seekers converging on Denver City. In the taverns of the mining-supply town, the argonaut army paused to eat, drink, look for grubstakes, and plan tomorrow's prospecting.

9

Then, exhausted by golden visions, they slept. After camping for weeks, emigrants welcomed the opportunity to sleep under a roof, even if it meant bedding down on a tavern floor or a billiard table.

Food service was no better than sleeping facilities. Old, heavily salted meat, beans, and hard bread were served with monotonous regularity. "There are no cooks in this country," Louis Simonin complained during his 1867 visit to Denver. He also noted the frontier predilection for washing down meals with "the sacramental glass of whiskey."[16]

By 1860 Denverites could choose from a wide range of imported whiskies, wines, champagnes, bitters, and liquors as well as lager from Denver's own Rocky Mountain Brewery. As alcohol brought a steady and high return in proportion to purchase and freighting costs, grocers, druggists, butchers, bakers, and dry goods firms as well as saloonists dealt in wet goods. One 1864 freighter devoted all of his eighty wagons to spirits, including sixteen hundred barrels of whiskey and twenty-seven hundred cases of champagne.[17]

Well-stocked saloons, with their Romanesque arch windows and corbeled brickwork, gave the town an aura of permanence and prosperity. Although others would join Lavinia Porter in condemning the prominence and prevalence of Denver's saloons in the years to come, these taverns reflected Denver's emergence as the stagecoach capital of Colorado Territory. They also made growth possible by providing drink, food, and shelter to the pioneers arriving at the confluence of the Platte River and Cherry Creek. Along these converging waterways and the stage routes that followed them, saloons offered many goods and services unavailable elsewhere during the years before self-proclaimed Denver City became a city in fact. Denver, like many other frontier communities, was weaned on the multifunctional saloon.

Chapter 2
THE MULTIFUNCTIONAL
FRONTIER SALOON

"A most forlorn and desolate-looking metropolis," is how the Boston journalist Albert D. Richardson described Denver upon his arrival by stagecoach in 1859. After crawling out of the stage, Richardson and his fellow journalist, Horace Greeley of the *New York Tribune,* found themselves surrounded by a crowd wearing slouch hats, tattered woolen shirts, and trousers sagging with knives and revolvers. Saloons emptied and the crowd thickened as word spread that "Go West" Greeley had come to town.[1]

Stiff and sore from the bone-shaking stage trip, Greeley and Richardson rented rooms in the Denver House. In that dirt-floored resort, Greeley found that a guest was "allowed as good a bed as his blankets will make." The charges, he added, were "no higher than at the Astor and other first-class hotels, except for liquor—twenty-five cents a drink for dubious whisky, colored and nicknamed to suit the taste of the customers."[2]

In the morning, Greeley sent to New York a dispatch in which he complained of the incessant clamor of all-night gamblers and of the inconvenience of dodging bullets fired by drunks. When the Denver House crowd asked the journalist to make a speech, he gave them a temperance lecture. The swizzling of drinks and shuffling of cards stopped momentarily while the patrons listened in respectful silence. But when Greeley returned to Denver several days later after his tour of Gregory Diggings, he found that his sermon had bounced off its targets. He shot off another widely quoted dispatch to the *Tribune* concerning Denver City and its saloon society:

> Prone to deep drinking, soured in temper, always armed, bristling at a word, ready with the rifle, revolver or bowie knife, they give law and set fashions which, in a country where the

11

regular administration of justice is yet a matter of prophecy, it seems difficult to overrule or disregard. I apprehend that there have been, during my two weeks' sojourn, more brawls, more fights, more pistol shots with criminal intent in this log city of one hundred and fifty dwellings, not three-fourths completed nor two-thirds inhabited, nor one-third fit to be, than in any community of no greater numbers on earth.[3]

Horace Greeley's complaint about the saloon-infested town was a common one. His traveling companion, Richardson, was also repulsed by the "many rude shanties for the sale of whiskey and tobacco" and wrote that "gambling and dissipation were . . . universal." William Hepworth Dixon, a British visitor to Denver in 1866, likewise complained that "as you wander about these hot and dirty streets, you seem to be walking in a city of demons. Every fifth house appears to be a bar, a whisky-shop, a lager-beer saloon; every tenth house appears to be either a brothel or a gaming house; very often both in one." Libeus Barney, a pioneer Denver taverner, claimed that every third building in the raw mining capital was a groggery.[4]

These critics exaggerated the number of saloons (see table 5) and also overlooked the town's reliance on saloons not only for social life but also for political, economic, and even religious activities. Saloons offered patrons far more than a nickel beer. They provided the cultural and social life of the French *salon,* the civic and political benefits of the Teutonic *saal* or public hall, the elegance of the Spanish *sala,* or parlor, and the sedate, private man's world of the British pub. Until government, churches, schools, banks, libraries, hospitals, theaters, museums, and other institutions became well established, the saloon served as a multifunctional institution.

In Denver's early years, saloons served as community centers where the provisional and permanent governments for Denver City and Jefferson Territory (the extralegal predecessor of Colorado Territory) were conceived, chartered, constituted, and housed during their early years. Taverns also doubled as clubs, hotels, restaurants, bakeries, hospitals, museums, banks, information centers, and gathering places. Denver's first church services and first theater performances were held in drinking halls. Behind tavern doors, men marketed town lots, traded mining claims, and grubstaked miners. "It is to be remembered," Jerome C. Smiley emphasized in his definitive history of nineteenth-century Denver, "that in these years the 'business' carried on in many of these 'business houses' was transacted over saloon counters."[5]

Saloonkeepers endeavored to meet as many of the needs and desires of their patrons as possible. "I flatter myself that I can please anyone," advertised Edward Jumps of the Criterion. David Hoyt's Pioneer promised to dispense choice wines, liquors, cigars, and other goods "in a scientific manner."[6] Operating both over and under the counter, tavernkeepers could tell a fellow where to find a girl, a bed, a job, or the latest gold strike.

Of course, the functions of any given saloon might change frequently.

Apollo Hall, a saloon and billiards hall housed in a two-story frame building erected in June 1859, provides a good example. Two months after its opening the Apollo made its debut as a hotel. The next month, on September 15, this Larimer Street establishment staged a grand opening ball offering five-dollar dinners and dancing to the "best music available." This drinking, billiards, sleeping, dining, music, and dance hall became Denver's first theater in October of 1859, when miners' candles were stuck into the walls and crude benches set up in the upstairs hall. Apollo Hall also accommodated churchless Presbyterians who met there in 1860 despite rattling billiard balls, drunken commotion, and occasional gunfire from the bar below. When the hubbub became unbearable, ministers led their flocks in the temperance hymn:

> There's a spirit above and a spirit below,
> The spirit of love and the spirit of woe.
> The spirit above is the spirit divine,
> The spirit below is the spirit of wine.

The zenith of the Apollo's life came in September of 1860 when townsfolk gathered there to draft a municipal constitution establishing the "People's Government of the City of Denver."[7]

Saloons housed many early religious services, since no churches were built until 1860, when a small Southern Methodist church and a Catholic chapel were completed. Years, even decades, passed before other denominations could afford their own buildings. Meanwhile, the Criterion Saloon served as a church for both Reverend John M. Chivington's Methodists and Reverend John H. Kehler's Episcopal flock, although one of Father Kehler's parishoners recalled that it was an ungodly place:

> On the first Sunday the gambling was carried on on the first floor while preaching was proceeding on the second. The flooring was of rough boards with wide cracks between them, and every word uttered by the occupants of the saloon, including those at the gaming tables, was as plainly heard by the congregation as the sermon. On the next Sunday the gambling was suspended for an hour while the preaching proceeded, which was considered quite a concession for that time.[8]

The records of Father Kehler's parish suggest the difficulties of churches in frontier towns. Of the first twelve burial services that he conducted, five of the departed had been shot, two were executed for murder, one shot himself, and one died of alcoholism. Murders at the Criterion, Cibola Hall, Mountain Boys, Louisiana, St. Charles, Adler's, and Club House saloons accounted for almost half of Denver's homicides in 1859 and 1860.[9]

The Reverend George Washington Fisher, the settlement's first Methodist preacher, found that saloons were powerful competition. After attracting only a handful of listeners while a much larger congregation attended a Sunday-morning faro game in the rum hole across the street, Reverend Fisher began preaching in saloons, reportedly from the text "Ho, every one that thirsteth, come ye to the waters, and he that hath no money, come ye, buy, and eat; yea, come buy wine and milk without price." Churchgoers may have found this sermon unconvincing, since signs on the tavern wall read "No Trust," "Pay as You Go," and "25cts. a drink."[10]

Many congregations borrowed saloon halls as their meeting places and sometimes used the bar as an altar and the bar's pianist as a choir director. Yet most churches found little use for groggeries once they had their own buildings. "The saloonist," grumbled the *Rocky Mountain Presbyterian,* "is, in one sense, if in no other, in the advance of our civilization in the West. He has time to ruin scores of men before the advance guards of the church arrive."[11]

Commercial banks were even slower than churches to establish themselves on the frontier. Two banks opening in 1860 proved to be short-lived. The Kountze Brothers Bank (later Colorado National Bank), established in 1862, and the First National Bank of Denver, organized in 1865, survived, but no others opened between 1865 and 1870. Easterners with capital were reluctant to finance banks in the new West, where inflation, a society of transient borrowers, lack of law and order, and a dearth of investors made banking risky. The banks that did exist in pioneer Denver were primarily gold buyers, not moneylenders.

In this capital-short frontier town, many miners and small businessmen turned to the saloonkeeper for cash. "Uncle Dick" Wootton claimed that about nine-tenths of the arrivals during the winter of 1858–59 were cash-hungry. Many of them sought to borrow money from Wootton, who accepted ox teams as collateral and charged interest as high as 20 percent a day. "This was a matter of such frequent occurrence," Wootton recalled, "that lending money in this way became a part of my business."[12]

The use of saloons as banks continued long after the territorial era. Immigrant groups in particular relied on tavernkeepers for exchanging foreign currency for American money, for depositing and withdrawing cash and other valuables, and for cashing checks. Louis Schmidt's Bank Saloon at Fifteenth and Market streets, for example, was precisely that. During the 1880s and 1890s, Schmidt's saloon cashed checks, handled foreign currency exchanges and rented safety deposit boxes. Schmidt's saloon was ideally suited for banking, since it had been the old Colorado National Bank building before that bank relocated in 1882.

In the saloonkeeper's safe, regulars might keep their savings and other valuables. Some liquor houses maintained letter boxes for regulars and posted notices, business cards, and want ads. Inside saloon doors (Denver's climate precluded extensive use of the swinging batwings), a tippler might find almost anything. Liquor houses tried to provide all of the comforts of home, from washboards to bathtubs.

The Frontier Saloon

Of all American institutions, the saloon was the quickest to move west with the people. In the first waves of frontier settlement, Americans left in their wakes schools, churches, city halls, banks, and other institutions. Saloons, however, sprouted quickly along the western trails, where they often became the nuclei of new towns.

While traveling to the Colorado gold diggings in 1859, Horace Greeley, editor of the *New York Tribune,* encountered a tent marked "GROCERY" but selling mostly wet goods. Greeley woke the proprietor from his nap between two whiskey barrels. He had no crackers, bread, or ham but told Greeley, "I have got some of the best whiskey you ever seen since you was born!"

Denver Public Library, Western History Department

Colorado Historical Society

Dozens of roadhouses like Pat Kelly's lined the Cherokee, Platte River, Smoky Hill, and Arkansas River trails into Colorado. The Cherokee and Smoky Hill trails brought emigrants into Denver along Cherry Creek, which was bordered by a series of roadhouses. Only two of these inns survive.

Thomas J. Noel photo

The Seventeen Mile House (above) is now a private residence in suburban Douglas County. The huge cottonwood beside the house supposedly hides the grave of an early patron who was murdered there.

Nancy Working Mendelsohn Collection

The Four Mile House, located four miles southeast of downtown Denver, dates from 1859, when two California miners built it near the Denver crossroads of the Colorado gold rush. It thrived as an inn for argonauts, emigrants, and other travelers and became a stagecoach stop. The place was converted to a farmhouse after the arrival of the railroads. An unknown artist sketched it around 1885 when it was the farmhouse of Levi and Millie Booth.

Thomas J. Noel photo

Despite brick and clapboard additions over the years, Four Mile House still rests partly on its first foundation—a huge cottonwood trunk spanning a dirt cellar. The oldest building in Denver, its exterior is made of Cherry Creek mud mortar and hewn ponderosa logs with full dovetail notching. Today this pioneer roadhouse has been converted to a museum and historic park. The photograph below shows the structure in 1977 just before restoration.

Denver's mile houses were among dozens of roadhouses catering to thirsty emigrants crossing the Great Plains. Augustus A. Hayes, a correspondent for *Harper's Magazine* who came to Colorado along the Arkansas River route, reported that traffic halted at resorts such as this one offering gin fizzes.

Hayes warned easterners traveling on the dry, dusty stage runs that westerners might offer them strange liquids with propositions such as "Stranger, do you irrigate?"

"STRANGER, DO YOU IRRIGATE?"

These roadhouses first served the immigrant wagons and many later became stage stops. Most of them vanished with the railroad era but a few have survived to refresh automobile tourists.

As the most common and commodious public buildings in many new frontier towns, saloons housed a wide variety of social and political activities. Miners descended on Denver watering holes, which offered women as well as whiskey.

The Old Capitol.

LEGISLATURE MEETS HERE.

MOVING THE CAPITOL.

The Colorado Territorial Legislature, which was born in Uncle Dick Wootton's grog shop, continued to meet in saloons for years. At the promise of more generous accommodations and libations, the legislators were likely to move their sessions.

A. A. Hayes, a correspondent for *Harper's magazine* and author of *New Colorado and the Santa Fe Trail,* visited Colorado City in the 1870s and found "the state-house still is standing. Tradition states that it contained three rooms: in one the members met, in one they slept; the third contained the bar! In the course of the proceedings a motion was made to transfer the seat of government to Denver." One of the legislators of 1862 told Hayes, "We carried our point because we had the best wagon, and four mules and the most whiskey."

Among those who came to Colorado to gamble with pick and pan rather than cards and dice, capital was also in great demand. And since alcohol was generally sold for cash on the frontier, miners looking for grubstakes often approached saloonkeepers. Not only were tavernkeepers lenders, but they also often held onto gold dust or cash for their customers after deducting bar bills from the deposited account. As a banker, the mixologist offered warmer hospitality, longer business hours, and liquid fringe benefits that conventional bankers could not match. When a customer was in arrears, the saloonkeeper told him to watch his pints and quarts, or "watch your Ps and Qs."

In Denver's first years, a pinch of gold dust became the standard price for a drink, although barkeepers with long fingernails sometimes collected extra. During gold dust transactions, some booze jugglers casually brushed their hair and washed out the proceeds later. Saloonkeepers could also collect tidy dividends when sweeping up their bars. Libeus Barney, who had little luck panning for gold up in the hills, found that the floor of Apollo Hall was a gold mine. Employing a pan and a turkey-feather broom, he extracted from the dirt, debris, and tobacco cuds $13.56 in gold dust.

At least one saloonkeeper doubled as an insurance agent. Edward Van Endert, coproprietor of Mozart Hall, advertised in the 1871 *Rocky Mountain Directory and Colorado Gazeteer* as the Denver salesman for Germania Life Insurance. Aiming his pitch at immigrants, he claimed that the Germania policy covered policyholders "traveling to & residing in Europe" and claimed that Germania was "the only American Company which has established agencies throughout Europe."[13]

If one saloonkeeper insured early Denverites, others served as physicians. Before the arrival of the patent-medicine salesman with his wagonload of cure-alls and the physician with his black bag, saloonkeepers dispensed whiskey for everything from snake bites to impotency, from bullet holes to mountain fever. Richard Townshend, an Englishman, reported the use of Dowd's Twenty Mile House on Cherry Creek as a hospital. A gunshot victim was laid on the bar counter under a smoky petroleum lamp and surgery was performed with a razor. Whiskey served as the anesthetic for both patient and surgeon.

Alcohol was a widely used health aid. It was the key ingredient of many nineteenth-century patent medicines. However, if brewery advertisements could be believed, drinkers had no need for other elixirs. "Invalids seeking health and strength," one 1870 newspaper ad announced, "are recommended by all physicians to drink Denver Ale Brewing Co's Ale and Porter," while Neef's later touted one of its beers as "Neef's Red Cross Malt Tonic."[14] Alcohol may have been safer than Denver's early drinking water, which came from the waste-filled Platte and Cherry Creek, from wells often adjacent to outhouses, and from the irrigation ditches that guttered city streets. The idea of alcohol as medicine became institutionalized in drugstore liquor licenses, sanctioned by both Denver's early ordinances and the first session of the state legislature.[15]

As the arena for much violence, saloons sometimes served not only as makeshift hospitals for injured patrons but also as mortuaries for dead ones. When James A. Gordon got roostered and shot John Gantz in 1860 for refusing a drink, cabinetmaker John J. Walley was called into the Louisiana Saloon to measure the deceased. As Denver lacked an undertaker at the time, Walley also wound up putting the dead man on ice, making the coffin, and burying him. Other barroom murders brought Walley so much business that he became Denver's first undertaker. Walley, they joked in saloons, buried many a corpse but never a coffin while transplanting people from barrooms to the boneyard. Walley also invoked squatter's rights to take possession of the city cemetery. This cemetery was better known as Jack O'Neil's Ranch, in memory of a popular bartender buried there, and it has since been converted to a park and botanic gardens. Saloons supplied Walley not only with corpses but with funeral expenses: Albert Nelson collected thirty-two dollars from his patrons to bury one pauper in the late 1870s.[16]

Shelter as well as dubious health care was furnished by early-day Denver saloonkeepers who liked to call their places houses. Inside, men might pay a quarter to sleep on sawdust floors or a dollar for the privilege of sleeping in a chair. These houses devoted most of their interior to bar space, but surrendered some back and upstairs rooms for sleeping. Some proprietors chalked off floor space at closing time and by dawn each of these spaces might house several snoring strangers. The less fortunate slept outside under wooden sidewalks, in empty barrels and boxes, in barns, stables, and outhouses.

Federal manuscript censuses reveal that quite a few saloonkeepers housed boarders. Many of Denver's early taverners were married men whose wives and children helped to make a home for the predominantly male, young, unmarried, transient miners. The saloonkeeper, his wife, and his children were very important in providing financial and occupational advice, health care, and company for the lonely young bachelors who had left their parents and sweethearts back in the states.[17] For example, the 1870 manuscript census lists Irish-born Patrick O'Connell as the proprietor of the Missouri House. Here O'Connell lived with his Irish-born wife, Catherine, and their seven children, ranging from sixteen-year-old Michael to four-year-old Mary. Besides this sizable family there were thirty-two boarders who had responded to O'Connell's advertisement that his house excelled at "everything pertaining to Hotel and Saloon keeping" and had on hand the best wines, liquors, ale, beer, and cigars.[18]

The ebb and flow of frontier populations washed many of the sick, indigent, handicapped, homeless, unemployed, and shiftless into Denver. The promise of gold, silver, and a salubrious climate made high, dry Denver particularly attractive to the poor and the sickly. The boom-and-bust mining cycles and the national depressions of the nineteenth-century economy also dumped many unfortunates into the Mile-High City, including worn-out miners from the hills who retreated to Denver to recover or to die.

From the beginning, many of the indigent approached tavernkeepers for handouts. In 1859, according to "Uncle Dick" Wootton, "There were hundreds of bitterly disappointed men who seemed to have come to Colorado thinking they could pick up gold nuggets almost anywhere, who found it difficult to pick up a square meal once a week. I fed a great many of them and did that much, at least, towards building up the city." "Uncle Dick" claimed that his Western Saloon and Hotel "failed financially for the reason that neither the manager nor myself could understand that only men who had money had a right to eat." Wootton concluded, "Our house was well patronized but in view of the fact that most of our patrons were free boarders I suppose it is not surprising that we did not make a success of the hotel business."[19]

On December 3, 1872, editor Byers of the *Rocky Mountain News* made an appeal for public assistance for the less fortunate, who continued to rely on tavernkeepers: "For six weeks past a stranger and invalid has been upon the hands of Gus Potter, of the Metropolitan Restaurant, Blake Street. He seems to be entirely destitute, and has cost Mr. Potter five or six dollars per day. This is an onerous and oppressive tax upon any citizen. The man should be taken in charge and comfortably provided for by either the council or city authority."

In frontier communities providing little or no charity and welfare, the men in the white aprons often contributed not only food and lodging but also cash to unfortunates. When yellow fever, caused by bad water, ravaged Denver in the 1870s, for instance, saloonkeepers John Kinneavy and Frank Parker donated bar receipts to fever victims.

If saloons provided frontier housing and welfare, they also offered cultural benefits, including reading material, art, music, theater, dancing, gardens, zoos, parks, and museums. Twenty years before Denver opened a permanent, free public library, the Rialto Billiard Saloon advertised, "Latest papers always on hand to while away a leisure hour." Andy Stanbury's Tambien offered beer sippers "files of daily, sporting, and illustrated papers." Along with imported and domestic cigars, meerschaum pipes, tobacco, and California wines, M. W. Levy kept "eastern, Colorado and California papers always on file." Literary-minded pioneers might also seek out Colonel Cheney's, which boasted elegant desks and reading tables where customers could read or write letters home amid all the appurtenances of a first-class bar, including "chaste, costly pictures."[20]

Cheney's was not the only saloon to offer Denverites public art decades before an art museum existed. Henry Fuerstein's beer hall exhibited paintings on its walls, including the oil "Yosemite Valley." Art-minded patrons who liked the California landscape were invited to purchase two-dollar raffle tickets on it. Charles Stobie rented one of the upstairs rooms at Stanbury's Tambien, where some of his Colorado landscapes and Indian portraits were first exhibited and purchased for as much as one hundred dollars. After editor Byers of the *Rocky Mountain News* saw Stobie's paintings in the Larimer Street grog shop, he judged them "the most excellent and beautiful work in oil painting we have seen executed in this country."[21]

One of the most beautifully decorated rooms in the whole West, proclaimed the *Denver Daily Times* for June 11, 1873, was the Senate Saloon, whose walls were painted with "allegorical representations of the four seasons." If Denver's finer saloons touted their "chaste, costly art," lesser taverns prized their less chaste barroom nudes and portraits of presidents, pugilists, and military heroes.

Drama as well as art found an early home in Denver saloon halls. When the Apollo Hall gave the city its first theater performance in 1859, the proprietor reported that an audience of four hundred squeezed into the hall, demonstrating "the appreciation of art in this semi-barbarous region." Aficionados of saloon theater customarily asked the entire stage company downstairs for a drink at the end of each act. This custom, as historian Smiley noted, "often resulted in lowering the standard of artistic effects in the closing scenes of the drama. However, the ability of the audience to discriminate was usually befuddled itself after . . . between-acts adjournments to the regions below."[22]

Theater, burlesque, minstrel shows, girly shows, and other stage performances were attractions at various bars. Of the sixty-odd theaters in Denver between 1859 and 1876, nearly all were in saloons. Ed Chase operated three of the best-known theaters—Arcadia Hall, Cricket Hall, and the Palace—and promoted his shows by sending through the streets an omnibus loaded with a brass band and can-can girls. On summer evenings, one Denverite recalled, the windows of Chase's Palace were open and the "street for a block was lined with broughams, berlins, phaetons, surreys, and other vehicles occupied by entire families drinking in the strains of classic selections," which "drowned out the voices of croupiers, the whir of the roulette wheels and the clink of chips and gold at the tables."[23]

Like theater, music was performed in saloons, although the life of a beer-hall musician might be a short one. To protect themselves from gun-toting critics, the musicians of the Denver House built a sheet-iron cage; when the shooting began they would dive under this battlement. After the smoke cleared, they would pop up playing again. Many of these musicians drank up their wages at the bar. City father William Larimer recollected that "after getting about a quart of Taos Lightning each, they would be asleep, mentally at least; though muscularly they would keep on with the same old see-saw of the same old tune over and over again, while the click of glasses and the rattle of feet and the rustle of cards and the interchange of vapid oaths and loudmouthed threats set up an opposing din, in the befouled atmosphere."[24]

Tavern amusements ranged from Eureka Hall's freak museum to an exclusive dance club sponsored by the Broadwell House. The Diana Saloon featured Signor Franco, a stone swallower, and his more voracious companion, a sword eater. The Blake Street Bowling Alley billed itself as the "*ne plus ultra* of popular resorts." It boasted four bowling alleys, good music, free lunches, and a bar "with everything." Above and beyond all this was a nightly trapeze performance by "Professor" Wilson.[25]

Bowling games and shooting galleries could be found in a few bars, but the crack and crashing of billiard balls was standard music in many public drinking halls. As early as 1860, the International Billiard Saloon boasted five first-class tables, comfortable lounges and armchairs for spectators, large ceiling chandeliers, and plenty of "the fancy" employed at the slate and marble tables.

Perhaps the crowning contribution to culture in early Denver was a spectacle sponsored by the Criterion Saloon. The Criterion employed a petite acrobat known as Mademoiselle Carolista. Sometimes blindfolded, sometimes with a wheelbarrow, Mlle Carolista walked a tightrope suspended from the stage of the Criterion to a rear balcony. But her tightrope walk from the roof of the Criterion to a store across Larimer Street was a highlight in popular entertainment during Denver's first decade. As she tottered on the rope, townsfolk stood petrified below with mouths open and arms outstretched.

Beer gardens served as public parks and gardens during Denver's first two decades. As Smiley pointed out, "If anyone had suggested to [the city fathers at that time] the actual need for city parks on their plats, they would have concluded that a far greater and an immediate one existed for a small asylum for insane advisers."[26] Denver had no city park system until the mayoralty of Richard Sopris in the 1880s, no municipal zoo until 1896, when Mayor Thomas S. McMurray was given a black bear cub and asked the foreman of City Park to care for it, and no Museum of Natural History until 1900.

Nineteenth-century thirst parlors, like twentieth-century fern bars and taxidermy taverns, surrounded customers with potted plants and mounted animals. Liquor and cigar cases were filled with arrowheads and fossils, geodes and stamp albums. Customers could sip drinks and study collections of cowboy hats and Indian scalps, of butterflies and seashells, of weapons and pornography. Tipplers in their cups found company not only in tavern dogs and cats, but in caged birds and wide-eyed fish.

Some saloons resembled museums and even botanical gardens. Elitch Gardens, Denver's best-known and oldest amusement park, began life as John Elitch's Arapahoe Street restaurant. The most exotic of the early beer gardens was the Olympic Gardens, sometimes called the Denver Gardens.

The Denver Brewing Company owned this park, which opened in 1872 with the help of brewery president Joseph E. Bates, who was the mayor of Denver at the time. Situated on the cottonwood-shaded west bank of the Platte (underneath today's Larimer-Colfax viaduct), Olympic Gardens included a park and picnic pavilion, a freak museum, a mineral exhibit, and a zoo of Colorado wildlife years before the city government provided such amenities. Omnibuses carried Denverites out to the gardens, which advertised, "Museum of Animals and Curiosities, Elegant Confectionaries, fruit, ice cream, lemonade, etc. Bar supplied with choice wines and liquors. The grounds are laid out in walks and carriage drives, so that the parties riding can visit all parts of the grounds without leaving their carriages, and footmen without crossing carriage roads. Full brass and string band will be in attendance. NO IMPROPER CHARACTERS ADMITTED!" In the heart of the city, Atlantic Hall promised patrons "a cool retreat with green, growing trees, flowers, and everything pleasant," including free lunches and twenty-five-cent quarts of lager beer.[27]

The National Park, a beer garden on Champa Street, featured a ballroom, a skating park, a large collection of animals, and a formal garden. This haven in the bleak, treeless town promised that everything within was conducted with "the highest regard for order and decorum." Claiming to be "the resort for the first society of the city and country," the National Park advertised good beer, good music, and good dinners as well as "games, exercises and amusements of all kinds."[28] For both play and work the town resorted to taverns.

The saloon's multifunctionalism was due to both the lack of other institutions and to the keen competition among the 270 taverns known to have existed in Denver during the territorial era. To attract customers, saloons attempted to outdo each other in offering novel goods, useful services, and unique entertainment.

Chapter 3
SALOON SOCIETY

Racing an unexpected October 1873 blizzard into Denver, a tiny woman urged her pony through tossing waves of prairie grass to a hill overlooking the Queen City of the Plains. Later she wrote to her sister in England:

> The great braggart city lay spread out, brown and treeless, upon the brown and treeless plain, which seemed to nourish nothing but wormwood and the Spanish bayonet. The shallow Platte, shriveled into a narrow stream with a shingly bed six times too large for it, and fringed by shriveled cotton-wood, wound along by Denver, and two miles up I saw a great sandstorm, which in a few minutes covered the city, dotting it out with a dense brown cloud.

Not only this brown cloud darkened Denver. Isabella Bird wrote further that an inordinate number of grogshops overflowed with "the characteristic loafers of a frontier town, who find it hard even for a few days or hours to submit to the restraints of civilization." In another letter she called whiskey the cause of most of Colorado's evil and violence.[1] Denver's many open saloon doors gave the city a boozy air that disgusted Isabella, just as it had disgusted Lavinia Porter and Horace Greeley a dozen years earlier.

Others also viewed the ubiquitous "dreadfalls" as fountainheads of evil. After arriving in 1859, William Newton Byers, Denver's first newspaper editor, kept a stern eye on the settlement's tippling houses. This proved to be a courageous undertaking. When he wrote unflattering editorials about the barroom crowd below his *Rocky Mountain News* office in the attic of "Uncle Dick" Wootton's Tavern, they sent bullets through the ceiling. Byers added extra floor planking, armed his staff, and decorated his office walls with notices of vigilante meetings.

Violent objections to the law-and-order *News* editorials continued nevertheless. On his first day in Denver, Presbyterian minister A. T. Rankin saw the saloon bunch attempt to murder Byers; and afterward he wrote about Denver's deplorable public morals. He reported that men who were moral and even churchgoers in the states profaned the Sabbath, gambled, and drank to excess. The Reverend attributed disturbances such as the attempted murder of Byers "to the drinking and gambling houses."[2]

After such episodes, editor Byers and other social critics redoubled their efforts to identify and condemn the frontier town's disreputable elements. One of the easier ways to sort society was to equate troublemakers with certain saloons, as the *News* did in 1860 by identifying Byers's assailants and the town's leading troublemakers as the Criterion Saloon crowd. In retaliation, patrons escorted Byers at gunpoint to the Criterion to hang him, but proprietor Charles Harrison broke up the necktie party.

Despite this humiliation, Byers continued to censure doggeries. In an 1865 review of the International Billiard Hall, the *News* called it a gathering place of the depraved:

> Ye gods! What a gathering! The foulest blasphemies in the shrill treble of female voices, rang through the building, causing the heart of the sensible or sympathizing hearer to ache with pity for these creatures, whom to call women were an insult upon humanity. Frantic screams, oaths, curses and yells, filled the hall, while whiskey's foul breath enveloped the dancers in a smoky fog, through which the bleared eyes and bloated faces of frail women gleamed malignantly, defiantly, and most beastly.[3]

In the same article denouncing the International, the *News* mentioned that the elite of Denver hobnobbed at the Christmas ball at the Tremont House. The Tremont, the Broadwell House, the American House, and Fred Charpiot's "Delmonico of the West" courted a distinguished clientele who probably would never be encountered at the International or at the Guard Hall, which Byers once declared a den of "intolerable nastiness," whose "bare-faced and bare-legged abominations are tabooed in respectable society."[4]

Not only newspaper editorials but advertisements as well indicate that bars catered to specialized clientele from the very beginning. Elegant hotel saloons catered to respectable citizens, while ramshackle dives served the down-and-out. While Olympic Gardens warned "NO IMPROPER CHARACTERS ADMITTED!," the No. 6 Saloon and Eating House across Blake Street from the Elephant Corral advertised twenty-five-cent meals at all hours for "freighters from the plains, farmers from the country and everybody who wants a good meal." As early as 1858, when the common folk celebrated Christmas at "Uncle Dick" Wootton's Taos Lightning stand, the genteel reportedly assembled three miles down the river at Captain R. A. Spooner's ranch to feast on oxtail soup, buffalo tongue, roast duck, dried mountain plums, and champagne.[5]

Although lower-class bars were open to everyone, the wealthy preferred to go elsewhere. If a poor man happened upon a pretentious place, he would probably be discouraged from staying by high prices and the aloof clientele. Denverites could classify their taverns as two-bit, one-bit, or nickel saloons, depending on the price of beer. One-bit bars were further divided into short-bit (ten-cent beer) or long-bit (fifteen-cent beer) groggeries.

Even within individual bars customers were often segregated just as their ancestors had been in English pubs, colonial taverns, and the drinking houses of the new American Republic. Back rooms, secluded tables, and private parties had long characterized inns. The physical layout of a typical Denver saloon suggests that customers were also segregated within frontier saloons. These drinking halls were long and narrow, conforming to the original 25-by-125-foot town lots. Bigger saloons might be built on two lots, using an interior partition between the bar and the restaurant. In either case, the establishment tended to be longer than it was wide, and the rear of the structure was frequently divided into rooms, where an elite could gamble, drink, and socialize separately from the front-hall crowd. Even within the front room, however, the customers at the bar counter and at the booths or tables often represented two different groups. Solitary, regular drinkers clustered at the bar, while semiprivate groups often sought out their own table. Multiple-story drinking houses offered still further possibilities for segregating patrons. Nineteenth-century real estate and insurance atlases portray mazelike partitioning of saloons and mind-boggling possibilities for pigeonholing tipplers.

The reality of a wide social spectrum of saloons in early Denver is difficult to reconcile with the traditional concept of an egalitarian frontier society, where all sorts supposedly rubbed elbows in the saloon. In this mythical saloon democracy, mining magnates and penniless prospectors, cattle barons and cowboys, town mayors and town vagrants drank at the same bar and gloried in the same frontier fraternalism. Not until the appearance of women and class-conscious institutions such as churches and schools, some have argued, did class distinctions appear.[6]

This notion of an open, democratic saloon society is undermined not only by architectural compartmentalization within individual bars but also by the wide variety of public drinking places. In 1859, the one-year-old Cherry Creek settlement had thirty-one saloons, pool halls, boarding houses, and restaurants that served alcohol. There were more saloons per capita in Denver during the first years than in any other period in the city's history, as Denver historian Smiley noted. "In some localities," he reported, "they shouldered each other in rows, and from one week to another, through the months, night and day, their doors were never closed."[7] In 1860, thirty-five taverns served Denver's 4,749 residents. Twenty years later the city directory listed ninety-nine saloons and the federal census takers counted 35,629 Denverites. In other words, there were almost five times as many saloons per capita in 1860 as in 1880. With so many bars to choose from, early Denverites usually divided along classlines when they headed for their favorite thirst parlors.

Class cleavages among Denver's earliest settlers were evident from the widespread stereotyping of undesirables as "bummers." Editor Byers and other commentators often defined the "bummers" as patrons of certain saloons such as the Criterion, whose proprietor, the gambler Charlie Harrison, was considered the chief "bummer."[8]

While leading citizens stereotyped some elements of society as "bummers," they tended to describe themselves and other stable, moneyed, and propertied settlers as "pioneers." As early as 1872, they held "Old Settlers" picnics and began setting up organizations such as the Pioneers Association, the Society of Colorado Pioneers, and the Sons of Colorado. Wealth and whiteness as well as early arrival in Colorado were membership criteria. These pioneer aristocrats decorated each other with ribbons at their picnics and banquets. On death, they were buried in palatial mausoleums inscribed "PIONEER."[9]

Chief among this elite was Governor John Evans. He was appointed Colorado's second territorial governor in 1862 by Abraham Lincoln, whose presidency he had supported early. Evans had made a fortune in Chicago real estate and railroads and had been an alderman there. He was a temperate Methodist who had founded the Chicago suburb of Evanston, home of the Woman's Christian Temperance Union and a bastion of the antisaloon crusade. In Denver, which Evans pronounced Colorado Territory's "only tolerable place," he largely confined his activities to an elite circle that he helped to create. Shunning barroom sociability, the governor and his carefully chosen friends often met in his fine house on the outskirts of town at Fourteenth and Arapahoe streets.

One of the more socially conscious visitors to early Denver, Louis Simonin, exulted in his invitation to the Evans home. "The society was select and animated," this Frenchman reported, "and we conversed as in a Paris salon, or, shall we say, as in the drawing room of the most cultivated Americans." Simonin, who visited Denver in 1867, concluded that "the pioneers arrived with their families, their wives and children, and from the first day society was formed on the eternally enduring foundations."[10]

As Simonin's use of the word suggests, not every early settler was eligible for the coveted title "pioneer." One such example was William McGaa, who was living on the site of the present city with his Indian wife when General William H. Larimer claim-jumped the land to found Denver City. McGaa, who claimed he was a nobleman and the son of a lord mayor of London, was a founding member of both the Denver and Auraria Town

Companies. He reportedly named Wazee and Wewatta Streets after two of his Indian wives and named Glenarm Place for his family's estate in Scotland and McGaa (now Market) Street for himself.[11]

Some attempts were made to record McGaa's adventures. An Englishman, John White, visited Denver in the early 1860s and sought out McGaa, who often used the name of Jack Jones. The problem, White reported, was that McGaa was always "so uniformly and thoroughly drunk that his evidence could not be taken." One Sunday evening, White cornered McGaa in the Planter's House. "By some lucky chance," White found the old mountain man "in a state approaching sobriety." The English writer tried to draw him out, but McGaa kept "throwing such longing looks toward the hotel bar" that White finally obliged him.[12]

According to the custom of that day, an empty tumbler, a tumbler half full of water, and the liquor bottle were placed in front of the customer so that he could mix his own. "Mr. Jones," the Englishman found, "did not trouble the water at all; but filling the second tumbler quite full of undisguised whiskey, drank it off at a breath, and immediately became drunk as usual."

No longer responding to questions, McGaa poured forth furry-tongued tales which, White assured his British readers, showed "what manner of men, in reality, are Cooper's idealized 'Pathfinders.' " Pathfinder McGaa gushed out tales of the peaks and passes he had scaled, of the squaws he had loved, of the braves he had slain and scalped, of the deaths of all his old sidekicks, and of his dark foreboding that the day "was soon to come when old Jack Jones would go up, too."

McGaa was also called "a loafer, and sot and begger" who "lived from hand to mouth," by Ed Chase, the saloonkeeper, who probably saw a lot of the old mountain man.[13] Byers, Evans, and other city fathers regarded McGaa as an embarrassment. In 1866, the Denver city council agreed to rename McGaa Street Holladay Street, after the stagecoach line owner. McGaa, the unworthy tosspot, was banished from the ranks of the founding fathers.

Thus did respectable citizens struggle to put themselves above other early settlers such as McGaa and his "bummer" friends. As late as 1901, Denver's leading historian, Smiley, was still defensively contesting the "popular but altogether erroneous belief" that the city was founded "by the refuse of the older communities." Yet Smiley's own account of violent, American-born whites reveals major conflicts within the dominant culture. American-born whites, according to another leading historian, were thought to be among the most restless and unstable groups on the frontier.[14]

White frontier society segregated itself according to regional as well as class differences. The most common type of name for the early-day board-inghouse saloons were those of the different states—Missouri House, Kansas House, California House, Iowa House, Pennsylvania House, and so on. In such places, people from the states named tended to congregate, hoping to find others of a similar regional background and experience.

Newcomers from the same area established bonds with each other in the new society and often derided groups from other regions. Edward Chase, who set up a gambling resort with some fellow New Yorkers, declared that "a great deal of low scruff here from California" was responsible for much of the early lawlessness in Denver. Californians "seemed to consider themselves a superior class of beings," according to Chase, who attributed several of the early brawls and murders in Denver to disputes between California "self-risers" and the eastern greenhorns whom they derided as "Pike's Peak Skunks." Another disputatious faction among Denver's first townspeople, Chase reported, were the "Web Feet" from Oregon.[15]

Vermont-born saloonkeeper Libeus Barney castigated the Missourians, whom the Boston Brahman Francis Parkman had found fifteen years earlier to be objectionable and ill mannered. The first Denverites came from Mexico, South America, Europe, and almost every state in the Union, Barney reported, "yet a majority of the decidedly bad men hail from Missouri; daring, desperate and lawless characters; having no fear of God or man; genuine specimens of border ruffianism."[16]

Regional conflicts reached a zenith in 1860–61, on the eve of the Civil War. After a few barroom brawls and other incidents, many of the Southern contingent left to join the Confederacy. Those leaving ranged from Denver's first mayor, John C. Moore, to the gambler, gunman, and bar owner Charles Harrison. Civil War antagonism increased the tendency of Denver's first saloons to cater primarily to regional groups. In the chaotic new society, saloons provided a bond based on regional origin, a place to find or hear of old friends or meet new ones from the same state and perhaps even the same county or town. As the manuscript census rolls show, tavern boarders tended to come from the same state or region.[17]

Although many whites declared that "bummers" such as Harrison were the worst troublemakers, they reserved their harshest discrimination for nonwhites. Racial discrimination provided an obvious impediment to an egalitarian society. From the beginning, many white saloonkeepers ostracized nonwhites.

A black who dared to patronize the Criterion was probably killed by Charlie Harrison's first bullet but was filled with several more as he lay on the floor. Harrison told the sheriff the man had dared to ask for service and say that "he was just as good as a white man." If they escaped violence, blacks met ridicule. Billy Marchand advertised that his saloon's pet monkey would not "shake hands with a darkey," but only with "first rate Republicans."[18] Blacks, of course, were tolerated as saloon employees—as waiters, dishwashers, porters, cooks, janitors, and spittoon cleaners.

Confronted by discrimination and given chances for only the most menial employment in white-owned taverns, blacks opened their own saloons. Henry O. Wagoner, Sr., maintained a black household and tavern on Blake Street across from the Elephant Corral and advertised in the 1866 city directory:

> Have you ever thirsted say,
> Or been hungry (by the way?)
> Well, if so, I'll tell you then
> A place where all honest men,
> Get wholesome food at cheap rates—
> Oysters, pies, and butter cakes,
> Nuts of dough, Chicago kind,
> Even cider too,—d'ye mind?
> Right down Blake Street you'll find—
> H. O. Wagoner is the host,
> And to please all is his boast.

For blacks and other nonwhites, barroom segregation and denigration continued well beyond the frontier period. Rising Jim Crow sentiment throughout the United States forced blacks into ghettos and fostered criticism of their activities—especially drinking, which some regarded as a white privilege only. Yet black bars became one of the most common businesses within Afro-American neighborhoods. In Denver the area around the railroad tracks at the foot of Twenty-third Street was sometimes called the "Deep South." There the city's small black population found its own culture and escape from the prevailing white milieu.

White newspapers snickered at the peculiarities of the "Deep South" and sensationalized its problems. They also portrayed black bars as promoters of defiance and violence. Denver's most notorious nineteenth-century black criminal, Andrew Green, allegedly made a jail-cell confession that his life in Denver, his decision to commit crime, and his arrest all revolved around an upper Larimer Street saloon. After arriving in Colorado, the young Missourian found lodging in the G.A.R. bar and met a confederate there, with whom he planned to rob a streetcar. During the robbery, Green murdered the streetcar driver. Afterward, Green continued to haunt the G.A.R. until he was picked up there and jailed for drunkenness and carrying a concealed weapon. Someone recognized him on the chain gang as the murderer, and he confessed the crime. An estimated ten thousand Denverites gathered along the banks of Cherry Creek to witness Green's hanging, the city's last legal one. The prosecutor denounced the "vile resort known as the G.A.R. Saloon" and suggested that the initials stood for "Great African Resort." He then observed that rather than lose one honest streetcar man it "would be better to hang every man that ever entered the G.A.R."[19]

In 1895, nine years after the Green case, an outburst in the black community was also attributed to alcohol. The *Rocky Mountain News* reported that "drunkenness ran riot" in a dozen saloons on Larimer and

Market streets. When two blacks were arrested for insulting the police, "the tough element of negroes who make their headquarters at the disreputable houses of the row [came] out in force." As a crowd of five hundred gathered, an inebriated "gentleman of color" threatened an arresting officer: "Ye doan want to hit dis hyar coon agin wid dat club. To-morrow I'm goin' to see de number taken off you' helmet. I'll go to jail like a gentleman, but yo' just wait till I git out'n dat jail." [20]

In these and other nineteenth-century racial flare-ups, the press often attributed black unrest to alcohol rather than to any underlying social problems and racial injustices.

Poor as their position might be in the nineteenth-century city, blacks fared better than Orientals. If Coloradans regarded blacks as inferior human beings, they looked upon the Chinese as subhuman. The first Chinese, noted the *Colorado Tribune* on June 29, 1869, "came in yesterday, a short, fat, round-faced, almond-eyed beauty. . . . He appeared quite happy to be among civilized people." The Chinese were invited to Colorado by Governor Edward McCook, who told the 1870 territorial legislature, "If we can first avail ourselves of their muscle, we can attend to their morals afterwards." [21]

How Colorado's "civilized people" would attend to the morals of the Chinese soon became apparent. Anti-Chinese sentiment ran wild in the 1880s. Although xenophobia and the threat of cheap labor were the main motivating factors, a common excuse for discrimination against the Chinese was their opium dens. The opium parlor, like the saloon, became a rationale for ostracizing an undesirable group. Their use of opium, or "yellow booze," gave whites an excuse for persecuting, as "dirty Chinese" and "filthy heathens," a race whose major occupation was cleaning the clothing of their persecutors.

Even in their "Hop Alley" ghetto (the alley between Blake and Wazee streets from about Sixteenth to Twentieth streets) the Chinese were not left alone. The Anti-Chinese Riot started there in John Asmussen's saloon on Sunday afternoon, October 31, 1880. Asmussen testified later that two Orientals and a white were shooting pool when some drunks began taunting them. Asmussen tried to stop the race baiting and then helped the Chinese slip out the back door. Outside, the Orientals were attacked and beaten and Colorado's only major race riot began. Agitators accused the Chinese of provoking the Halloween violence, and as rumors swept the lower downtown area, some three thousand people gathered in the early-morning darkness to destroy the Chinese and their ghetto. Terrified Chinese hid in cellars and attics while the mob shouted, "Stamp out the yellow plague" and "Death to the chinks," according to the *Rocky Mountain News*. Rioters looted and burned Hop Alley, beating some Orientals and lynching an elderly washerman, Sing Lee.

While the police and fire departments balked, some of the white Hop Alley residents, primarily saloonkeepers, gamblers, and prostitutes, tried to defend the hapless Chinese. Saloonkeeper James Veatch sheltered refugees in his Red Lion Inn. Gambler Jim Moon took in a Chinese friend and then confronted the mob storming his front door. "This Chinaman is an inoffensive man, and you shant touch him, not a ———— one of you."[22] Moon's words and the mute eloquence of his leveled revolver dissuaded the mob. Lizzie Preston, a Market Street madam, herded four cringing Chinese into her parlor. When a deputy sheriff finally arrived, he found Lizzie and ten of her girls, armed with champagne bottles and high-heeled shoes, holding the crowd at bay.

Chinatown, the *Rocky Mountain News* gloated afterward, was gutted. "There was nothing left . . . and the rooms so recently the abode of ignorance, vice and shame contained nothing beyond the horrid stench emitted by the little wads of opium." The Chinese consul at San Francisco inspected the remains and estimated losses at a little over fifty-three thousand dollars, a sum for which his people were evidently never reimbursed.[23] Although the riot was spent, Denver's anti-Chinese bigotry was not. In the following years, Orientals were shot to death, attacked by mobs, and driven to suicide. Their elaborate funeral ceremonies were sometimes disrupted by jeering white gangs.

Existing amid persecution, poverty, and wretched living conditions, the Chinese depended heavily on opium. By 1880 the city had seventeen known opium dens, which were as basic to the Chinese community as saloons were to other Denverites.[24] Inside these "hop joints" the people of Hop Alley savored the sweet fragrance of dried poppy juice and dreamed of making their fortunes and returning to their families and their homeland.

In 1881, Denver passed an ordinance outlawing opium dens, thus denying the Chinese one of their few comforts.[25] Patronage of opium dens, like patronage of "bummer" or black bars carried a social stigma. And the crackdown on opium dens as a means of harassing the Orientals foreshadowed increasing hostility to the saloon as a resort of poor whites, blacks, immigrants, and transients.

The arrival of the railroads signaled a great influx of people, including many railroad laborers and vagrants who frequently gravitated to Denver's doggeries. Not since the days of '59 had saloons overflowed with such a migratory horde. "Beer halls," the press noted several weeks after the arrival in 1870 of the Denver Pacific Railroad, "are becoming quite numerous in Denver."[26] The reason for the proliferation of taverns was suggested by the names that some of them took: the Railroad House, Denver Pacific Dining Rooms, Union Depot Exchange Saloon, and Depot Saloon.

If the arrival of the railroads brought prosperity, it also brought in poor vagrants who swelled Denver's saloonhall society. Denver's leaders were no happier about the vagrants of the 1870s than they had been about the "bummers" of the 1860s. Nevertheless, the city became the regional stopover for soot-and-cinders transients.

When Mayor William Warner of Kansas City, Missouri, began a crusade to send undesirables packing, Byers editorialized in the *Rocky Mountain News*, "We warn any of the rogues who escape towards Denver that hemp is abundant in this city and that there are men here who are not afraid to use it." On another occasion the same newspaper complained that "they come hither by railway and doubtless as dead-heads in the character of paupers. . . . The great states of Missouri and Kansas ought to be able to take care of their own poor." Discouraging charity to these vagrants, the *News* claimed that the money they "collected in Denver by day was spent in low groggeries at night," that "the proceeds of charity were squandered at the beer counter."[27]

Despite the campaign against them, transients came by the boxcarload, often hopping off in the bums' jungle between the tracks and the South Platte River. In the summer, they camped out. In the winter, they came into town seeking the warmth of skid row. At free-lunch saloons, they tried to "jawbone" drinks and gorge themselves on meats, cheeses, baked beans, hard-boiled eggs, crackers, bread, and pickles.

Although not as numerous as the men, female tramps also arrived by rail. Lizzie Greer's story appeared in the *Denver Tribune* on November 8, 1885. Lizzie had "probably been a factory girl, and it was thought that her employer had been her destroyer." She had taken to drink and "had drifted away from all her friends." She lived "in the filth of alleys and stables and drank only what she could beg from one saloon to another," tipping up empty beer kegs in back of saloons "to drain out the last stale drop into her can and drink it with as much relish as if it were nectar."

Several gamblers took Lizzie in and tried to rehabilitate her, an endeavor described by the *Denver Tribune*.

> She was very drunk, and very dirty; her face was so begrimed that her identity was almost concealed, and her eyes were swollen shut from the long, drunken stupor she had been in. Some charitably disposed persons picked her up . . . and endeavored to make something of the girl besides the low, drunken thing they found groveling in the mud.
>
> They gave her a warm bath, keeping her in the water a long time so that the dirt might soak off, and then they went to work on her long tangled yellow hair. When it was combed and coiled it was beautiful; full of changing lights, soft and wavy, and pretty to look at. The girl was pretty, too, when the dirt came off, and she was neatly dressed and sober.

This Pygmalion scheme failed. Lizzie returned to the bottle and resumed spending her nights in stables or in jail. Her days were devoted to a quest for liquor until the end came one freezing night in a coal yard next to the Windsor Hotel on Larimer Street.

Denver journalists, like other nineteenth-century social critics, tended to equate poverty and vagrancy with saloon going. "The throngs of men who line our streets and fill our concert saloons," editor Byers once postulated, "are pursued by infirmity of purpose which drives them from the active ranks of life, and makes barroom fixtures out of them who might adorn society under better circumstances."[28]

The saloon-going poor could not expect much help from Denver's Charity Organization Society, which coordinated the city's public and private social services after 1889. This society condemned "indiscriminate alms-giving" and tried to distinguish the "worthy" poor from the "unworthy." Drinkers would most likely be placed in the latter category.[29]

The railroad carried thousands of transients through Denver each year, reinforcing the "turnstile town" pattern established during the gold rush when fewer than five thousand of the estimated forty thousand argonauts reaching Cherry Creek in 1859 could be counted as 1860 Denver residents. The high ratio of floating population to residents declined over the years but remained significant. Fifty years after the gold rush, a Denver newspaper estimated that the city had an average floating population of eighteen thousand.[30]

After 1870, the Queen City's expanded rail network relied in part on Denver's floating proletariat for labor. By 1880, the Denver and Rio Grande alone was shipping hundreds of men every month from Denver to various railroad construction sites. These transient railroad workers, as well as sheep herders, stockmen, traveling salesmen, and migrant laborers made Denver a spree city where, as Isabella Bird noted in 1873, "men go to spend the savings of months of hard work in the maddest dissipation."[31]

Bar proprietors as well as their patrons were highly mobile. During the nineteenth century, Denver's visitors seldom found the same saloon and the same saloonkeeper in the same location for two years in a row. Transient saloonkeepers catering to transient clienteles characterized bar life throughout the nineteenth century. While Denver evolved from a frontier crossroads to a major metropolis, saloonhall social life remained a mainstay for the drifting masses.

The mobility of this society affected the nature of its saloons. Rather than catering primarily to an established, perennial neighborhood clientele, many Denver bars sought to attract the thousands of travelers passing through town. In the summer, the city and its saloons were crowded with transients. In the winter, unemployed miners from the mountains and agricultural workers from the plains gravitated to Denver, where they basked in the warmth of potbellied saloon stoves.

All of the groups socializing in saloons—"bummers," blacks, Orientals, railroaders, railroad transients, miners, stockmen—generally had their preferred watering holes. Then as now, tipplers usually chose to bend elbows with people of similar racial, occupational, and regional backgrounds. Particularly in the chaotic new frontier society, saloons served as gathering places where men could find or hear of old friends and meet new ones from their former homes, pick up occupational news and opportunities, and relax comfortably with their own kind. Tipplers cared little that they and their bars were stereotyped and condemned as "bummer," "hobo," "skid row," "Chink," and "nigger."

In subsequent decades, when foreign-born immigrants became more numerous, they would follow the same pattern of congregating in the taverns of their countrymen. This social segregation and stratification became more apparent as protection-seeking bar owners and vote-hungry politicians began to organize saloonhall society politically.

Chapter 4
SALOON POLITICS

Before city halls, county courthouses, and statehouses were built in frontier capitals such as Denver, settlers commonly met in saloonhalls to create and conduct their first governments. As the first, largest, and most ubiquitous public meeting places, saloonhalls were birthplaces of self-government and housed city councils, courts, and legislatures in their early years.

Government not only found a home in the liquor houses but also developed close ties with the liquor men during the territorial period. Indeed, reformers spent much of the three decades following Colorado statehood trying to get the saloon out of politics and then to get the bars out of business altogether.

In 1859, when Denver was barely six months old, townsfolk convened in "Uncle Dick" Wootton's saloon to sever their ties with Kansas Territory. A constitution was drawn up, elections were held, Jefferson Territory was created, and a delegate was sent to Washington. Recognized by neither Kansas nor Washington, Jefferson Territory was a short-lived and ineffective creature. However, this initial effort at self-government helped nudge the federal government into establishing Colorado Territory two years later.

The infant legislature conducted its sessions in Apollo Hall, the Criterion, the Windsor, the White House, and other places until 1894, when the solons moved into the still unfinished state capitol building. Construction of the statehouse had been delayed numerous times, first until statehood came in 1876, then until a statewide referendum officially confirmed Denver as the capital city in 1881, and again until the resolution of a lengthy debate over landownership and the eventual voting of construction bonds.

After having had liquid refreshments available to them for years, thirsty legislators made arrangements to meet their needs in the new capitol building. Even as the legislature debated prohibition, the liquor lobby maintained a "lubricating room" in the capitol to keep "wet" legislators entertained and informed on the drink issue. (The tradition continues with the Colorado General Assembly, where the "Sunshine Laws" of the 1970s shone on the free beer ice box that the Adolph Coors Brewery has maintained at the statehouse.)[1]

Denver's municipal government was also created in saloonhalls. In September of 1860, townsfolk climbed the rickety staircase to the hall of the Apollo for the town meeting that created the "People's Government of the City of Denver." This provisional city government, although extralegal, oversaw the election of a mayor and city councilmen and the establishment of "People's Courts" to deal with the criminal activity that plagued the new town. These vigilante court sessions, whether held in bars or not, sometimes convened with intoxicated results, as in the trial of Charlie Harrison. An eyewitness reported that a group of men gathered under the jury-room window as darkness fell. The jurors hung a rope from the window and hauled up a basket "filled with grub, cigars and flasks of whiskey, which the jurymen took out of the basket and put into themselves."[2] Soon afterward, a fight broke out in the courtroom among the drunken jurors. Even after the sheriff called in the bailiffs to restore order, the jury could not agree on a verdict. The next morning they were discharged and Harrison was turned loose.

Perhaps with such trials in mind, one Denverite wrote a letter describing how the "People's Court" selected one of its judges. "Whiskey had reduced him to the starving point," Thomas Wildman confided to the home folks about the judge, "when some of his bummer friends apealed [sic] to the public that the old rule of kicking a man when he was down might be reversed here at Pike's Peak, so we elected him judge. He has now a clean shirt and part of a new suit of clothes [and] may be said to be a rising man."[3]

Despite such shortcomings, "Judge Lynch" and the "People's Courts" struggled to keep the infant municipal government honest. As a result, Councilman John Shear, a corpulent, dissipated gambler, was found one morning dangling from a cottonwood tree. Fastened to a nearby stump was a note: "This man was hung. It was proved that he was a horse-thief."[4]

Perhaps in the hope of recovering its dignity after such scandals, the Denver City government moved out of the Apollo and into a shack labeled City Hall. However, when the new city hall washed away in the 1864 Cherry Creek flood, the mayor and council returned to Apollo Hall. Saloons and other makeshift headquarters continued to house municipal government until a permanent city hall was completed at Fourteenth and Larimer streets in 1883.

Saloons not only housed government but also financed it. Frontier governments were desperate for revenue but frontier settlers balked at taxation. They would just as soon push on as pay up. This led Denver City and many other tax-hungry frontier towns to look to ubiquitous and thriving saloons as a tax base. In Leadville's early years, saloon fees provided two-thirds of that city's revenues. In another Colorado town, Silverton, liquor license revenues accounted for about 90 percent of the city's income.[5]

Denver's first city charter in 1861 gave the municipality authority "to license, restrain, regulate, prohibit and suppress tippling-houses, dram-shops, gambling houses, bawdy-houses, and other disorderly houses." Initially only gambling halls paid annual license fees of $50 to $100. By 1862, however, tavernkeepers were required to post a $150 to $300 bond and pay an annual license fee of $50 to $100, depending on whether they served just beer and wine or sold hard liquor as well. Four years later the license fee was raised to $200 for spirituous liquors and $140 for malt liquor. By 1875, Denver was collecting roughly $35,000 a year in liquor license fees. By 1900, liquor license revenue had risen to $215,538, which amounted to almost a fourth of the city's expenses that year.[6]

Soon after its creation, the territorial government also began charging all liquor outlets a $25 annual license fee. Saloons were also subject to the tariff on all merchandise that was "not the growth, manufacture or product of the territory." Gambling halls were taxed $2.50 per month "on each table or other appliance used for gambling." By 1889, the legislature's "high license" act raised saloon fees to between $600 and $1,000 per year.[7]

Bars became the most regulated private business. The government had the authority to approve or deny anyone's request to go into the liquor business. Once a request was approved, officials also regulated when and where the owner could open a saloon, and what, how much, and to whom he could sell. Denver City Ordinance Number One outlawed sidewalk and street gambling and liquor sales. Civic and business leaders complained that the gutter tumult created by these practices impeded traffic, scandalized visitors, and blocked access to reputable business houses.[8]

Ordinance Number One was only the opening shot of a battery of laws aimed at saloonists. An 1865 city council resolution outlawed the sale or gift of liquor to one Charles White, better known as "Crazy Charlie." Other drinkers were banned from taverns in 1885, when bars were required to hang in a conspicuous place a large sign reading "NO MINOR OR HABITUAL DRUNKARD ALLOWED HERE." Nine years later ladies were added to the dry list.[9] Ultimately, of course, the entire population was barred from patronizing saloons.

Some groggeries never closed, a fact that soon attracted the city council's attention. A midnight-to-six-in-the-morning closing law was passed in 1865, but this attempt to enforce nocturnal abstinence drew such a barrage of criticism that it was repealed. Passed again the following year, the night closing ordinance long remained a controversial and widely disregarded law. Even after policemen began ringing a loud midnight curfew bell, tipplers and taverners alike ignored attempts to establish a last call for alcohol.

Throughout the nineteenth century, reformers also struggled first to pass and then to enforce a Sunday saloon-closing law. Ultimately, saloon-keepers were more or less compelled to comply with this Sabbath law that presaged seven-day-a-week prohibition.

Other laws restricted the location of saloons. An 1889 statute forbade bars within five hundred feet of any school or church and the 1898 revised city charter forbade the awarding of licenses within four hundred feet of public parks or squares. Applicants also had to get written approval from the majority of property owners on the block where they proposed to open a saloon. Even then, city officials might arbitrarily withhold the license. A man could no longer determine where his saloon might be. That became the decision of his neighbors and the city council.[10]

Local governments were able to single out saloons for heavy taxation and discriminatory regulation because many voters regarded drink parlors as an evil or a public nuisance. The police power of the state was invoked to impose on this "nuisance" financial burdens and stringent restrictions. Taxing saloons, many felt, was taxing the wages of sin.

Throughout the nineteenth century, the forces of righteousness were often led by the *Rocky Mountain News*. Editor Byers, who had spearheaded the campaign against barroom "bummers," preferred hard candy to hard liquor, and he was not alone. Even before his arrival in April of 1859, prohibitionists had established a temperance club. Three years later the Independent Order of Good Templars, or "Water Tanks," launched a Denver chapter. As the cold-water army grew, it successively fought for higher license fees, midnight closing, Sunday closing, saloonless suburbs, and, ultimately, prohibition.[11]

At the election polls, liquor men found themselves unable to defeat mounting public pressure for stricter government regulation of their trade. So the liquor lobby began to use illegal tactics, including bribery, payoffs, and election fraud. By these tactics some saloonkeepers and associated gambling and prostitution interests played a major role in corrupting city government or in sustaining already corrupt officials.

Corruption became conspicuous when gambling hall operators attempted to undermine laws passed in the 1860s. Originally gambling was open and widespread in Denver. Many town fathers had amused themselves with poker games, using town lots for chips; they won or lost whole blocks during the course of a night's gaming. Gambling, reported Chicagoan John D. Young upon his arrival in 1860, was "the most extensive business carried on there and participated in by all classes of citizens." Richardson, the journalist, sat in on a Sunday morning session in 1859 at the Denver House, where the county probate judge lost thirty Denver lots in less than ten minutes of card playing and the county sheriff pawned his revolver for twenty dollars to bet on faro.[12]

Despite the prevalence of chance taking, the new governments, in their efforts to impose law and order, decided that gambling halls should be abolished. The 1866 legislature outlawed gambling and Denver also banned gambling, but the fine was so light—no less than ten dollars and no more than one hundred dollars—that it virtually licensed gambling.[13] These laws did, however, force some gamblers underground where they found it comfortable as long as the politicians and the police could be bought off and public scrutiny avoided. Gamblers also began to organize to protect themselves by participating in urban politics. The first "czar" of Denver's gamblers was tall, hawk-faced Edward Chase. Chase came to Denver at the age of twenty-two in 1860. For the next half century he made it his business to organize the underworld into a voting bloc whose support could be traded for protection of his numerous sporting houses.

"Big Ed" Chase had Denver's first billiard table hauled across the plains by ox team for his Arcadia on Blake Street. "I made the place as inviting as I could for the boys," Chase recalled years later, "but furniture was scarce in those days and they considered themselves fortunate if they had benches to sit on, while the card tables were covered only with woolen blankets."[14] Free lunches and nickel beers helped to bring in the masses, who kept Arcadia Hall roaring far into the night. Tall, immaculately dressed Ed Chase perched on a high stool with a shotgun across his elbow, surveying the room. Chase prided himself on keeping an orderly house, although lawmen persistently called his saloon disorderly.

In 1863, Chase and a partner, Francis P. Heatley, replaced the Arcadia with Progressive Hall, one of the city's largest and most impressive structures. Here Denverites gambled, drank, and enjoyed the burlesque and vaudeville of the Progressive's variety theater. Chase sold the Progressive in the mid-1860s when stagnation threatened Denver's future because easily recovered surface gold and the possibility of attracting the transcontinental railroad seemed to have disappeared. Along with many other Coloradans, Chase set out for the new boom town of Virginia City, Montana. When Montana's stern vigilantes cracked down on the sporting element, however, Chase headed back to Denver.

Upon returning, Chase and his younger brother, John, opened a new gambling house, the Cricket. The theater next door was added to the Cricket after Chase acquired it allegedly by giving the owner the twenty-five dollars he needed to get out of town. The Cricket soon became one of Denver's leading theaters and offered the adolescent city a chance to laugh at itself with hometown comedies. One was billed as "a terrible struggle between the runners of the American and Tremont House about an old Irish woman's carpet bag" and another advertised "Attention ye Lot Jumpers—Further disclosures of the contents of the City Sale will be made to-night at the CRICKET." Chase paid good money to attract performers such as Eddie Foy and Madameoiselle Marie, the "queen of burlesque."[15]

Evidently the Cricket was a lucrative operation. The 1870 federal manuscript census reported that Chase was worth over twenty thousand dollars. R. G. Dun and Company's Denver credit agent, in his confidential 1868 appraisal, described Chase as "a rich and clever man . . . sometimes good for $50,000 sometimes not so much." The agent added a note of caution for Chase's creditors: "Touch him lightly for a few weeks as he is indicted for assault and battery with intent to commit murder." The Dun reports for the early 1870s confided that Chase was pawnbroking as well as owning and operating a gambling den. "A notorious gambler," the Dun agent called Chase, "a hard man [who] keeps a lewd and dangerous place . . . a blackleg." Chase's wife evidently agreed. She sued for divorce after discovering that he kept a mistress at the Cricket. Margaret Jane Chase claimed that in 1874 her husband owned over seventy-five thousand dollars worth of Denver real estate, thirty thousand dollars in Saratoga, New York, properties, and one hundred thousand dollars in cash and personal effects.[16]

Even after settling with his wife, "Big Ed" could afford to erect the large, two-story Palace Theater that stood at Fifteenth and Blake streets well into the twentieth century. The Palace seated 750 burlesque fans and the adjacent gambling chamber accommodated 200. Besides a well-stocked bar, the Palace provided midnight suppers of roast beef, antelope cutlets, breasts of prairie chicken, and other delicacies. Chase's Palace was ostensibly a theater but the shows were primarily leg art. Waitresses alternately served drinks and performed in the chorus line, which ran continuously from 9:00 A.M. to 4:00 A.M. In curtained booths, wine girls served such prominent customers as United States Senators Edward O. Wolcott, Horace Tabor, and Thomas Bowen.

These three senators were not alone in relishing the city's "Wild West" attractions. Many politicians and businessmen wanted to keep Denver a wide-open town attractive to tourists, traveling businessmen, conventioneers, and the miners and ranchers of the hinterland. When residents of surrounding small towns came to Denver they often sought fun as well as business. "The weight of public sentiment as far as the businessmen of this city is concerned," declared a Denver magazine, "is against the closing of the gambling houses in this city."[17]

Despite the popular amusements he provided and his connections with leading politicians, Chase was arrested several times on gambling charges. Reformers and incumbent politicians eager to polish their reputations found the gambling ace an inviting target. "Big Ed" usually escaped conviction with the help of Denver attorney Mary F. Lathrop, a tiny Quaker. Chase insisted that he was not a professional gambler—only a proprietor who leased tables to gamblers under a system where neither party could be held responsible for gambling. By the time the police arrived, the renter could not be found and the owner could not be held for his tenant's crimes.

Chase's Palace was a murderous resort. The *Georgetown Courier* for December 6, 1888, reported one of many homicides there: "Another murder at the Palace Theatre, Denver. A.W. Munson shot and killed

Thomas Miller last Sunday night. From the amount of blood that has been spilled in that den, its floors must be of a gorgeous, gory red color."

Numerous arrests, sporadic crackdowns, and escalating liquor license and payoff fees all kept Chase politically active. He paid as much as twelve hundred dollars a year in license fees as well as payoffs. "Oh yes," he acknowledged just before his death, "I was held up often, but I never found it profitable to kick about it. . . . And as I grew older I knew better how to keep the law wolves off."[18]

"I did many things to help out my friends among the politicians in my long career," Chase explained delicately. "I had to do so to keep my friends and assume a proper degree of protection. Most of the candidates sought my help, but I made it a point to be pretty sure of the success of the man whose cause I championed. Possibly I did some things in the way of getting votes that the law did not sanction, but I went no further in that regard than the politicians themselves."[19] Behind these modest understatements stood the man who played a major although hidden hand in shaping Denver's political history in the nineteenth century.

Originally Chase had been openly involved in politics. He represented the first ward as city councilman from 1866 to 1869. After thus broadening his political education, Chase retired from public office but remained prominent among the backroom politicians of the Republican party, which dominated Denver politics. His specialty was organizing the large number of transients, prostitutes, street people, derelicts, gamblers, winos, and underworld denizens of the lower downtown wards into an army of voters. Very loose voting residence requirements made Chase's task easier. To qualify as a resident voter, a man needed only to live or be "accustomed to lodge" in his ward for ten days.[20] For a dollar and a drink, a large number of transients, who knew little and cared less about Denver politics, could be herded to the polls to vote for Chase's friends.

Ed Chase's council membership was not extraordinary—there was nearly always one saloonkeeper and often more on the city council. Among the saloon owners on the city council during the nineteenth century were John A. Nye, James M. Broadwell, Henry Fuerstein, Moritz Sigi, Philip Zang, J. A. McIntyre, David J. Kelley, Hartsville F. Jones, Jerome S. Riche, John Trankle, Peter Fidel, and James Doyle.

Like backroom politicians in other cities, quite a few of Denver's ward bosses operated out of saloons. Establishments such as the Fourth Ward Saloon, Guard Hall, and Walhalla Hall were political gathering places. Some of the voter registration booths and voting stations were set up in taverns. Saloons, complained the *Rocky Mountain News,* tried to dominate primaries and dictate elections in order to secure immunity from various laws. Calling this "the origin of the saloon power in politics," the *News* added that the saloon had become "a place where much of the ordinary political work is carried on."[21]

From the first election of 1861, when Denver was officially chartered, saloonkeepers attempted to orchestrate elections and keep the voters well disposed with free election-day libations. In the first official election of 1861, ballot-box stuffing was so pervasive that a second election had to be scheduled. But even in the second election, the press lamented, "We have never before seen, at one time in the streets of Denver, as many drunken men, as many fights, or as much boisterous rioting." By 1865, according to the city's leading nineteenth-century historian, Councilman Ed Chase and the gambling fraternity "had managed to exert political control of the municipality."[22]

When statehood came in the 1870s, the situation did not change. Even the 1876 statehood election was rigged. Governor Charles S. Thomas later expressed relief that the election had not been challenged. Prostatehood men "voted early and often," Thomas admitted. "Hack loads of voters visited every polling place, some of them making a second trip."[23]

During the territorial period, the saloon housed and influenced local self-government and, many have charged, corrupted it in the process. But as government officials showed a propensity for liquor and corruption from the beginning, it might also be argued that government corrupted the saloon. Doubtless some city officials initiated the common practice of collecting bribes—either in cash or in votes—from saloonkeepers in exchange for protection. At any rate, the close connection between politicians and saloonkeepers spawned persistent election fraud. Practically every Denver election from 1861 to 1908 was followed by newspaper stories of illegal voting practices.

In another sense, the undermining of Denver politics during the territorial period suggests that the city founded on a gamble for gold was increasingly reluctant to take chances. Gamblers and saloonkeepers, after initially taking their chances with government regulation and sporadic legal crackdowns, got into politics to protect themselves against prosecution. Politicians, who at first may have been willing to trust the electorate and the democratic system, increasingly aligned themselves with saloonkeeping ward bosses such as Ed Chase to ensure their election. In the coming years the bonds between the tavern and town hall would grow even more obvious and objectionable. Before delving further into their social and political activities, however, a look at the economic aspirations and achievements of the men behind the mahogany is in order.

Chapter 5
"THE CHEAPEST AND EASIEST WAY TO BECOME AN INFLUENTIAL MAN"

"The cheapest and easiest way to become an influential man and be looked up to by the community at large," wrote Mark Twain, "was to stand behind a bar, wear a cluster-diamond pin, and sell whiskey." America's most prominent frontier correspondent went on to say, "I am not sure but that the saloonkeeper held a shade higher rank than any other member of society."[1]

Twain's tongue-in-cheek appraisal of the mining frontier is only slightly overdrawn. Keeping a saloon was easier work than grubbing for gold, chasing cattle, busting sod, or laying railroad track. Most manual work was health wrecking and paid poorly. In Denver in 1873, carpenters and bricklayers made up to $5.00 a day but unskilled laborers and railroad workers made only $2.50. Miners averaged $3.50 a day. Many farmers lived in debt and poverty and eventually failed. Cowboys made only about $40.00 a month.[2]

Many of these poorly paid manual workers jumped at the chance to don the saloonkeepers's white apron, for that occupation held promises of a less strenuous life, the ability to set their own working hours, and the possibility of prospering in their own business.[3] For blue-collar workers, tavern proprietorship was a first step into the white-collar world and a whole new realm of entrepreneurial possibilities. Saloonkeepers seemed well aware of the dignity of their position. They sported luxurious mustaches and wore diamond stickpins, stiffly starched, shiny white shirts, and natty ties. If they could afford a bartender, the apron and the hard work were left to him.

Saloonkeeping, of course, was only one of many possible careers on the frontier, where men could start out or start out all over again in any one of a wide variety of occupations.[4] The frontier's relatively young population, its chronic labor shortage, and its many new communities made it an area of high occupational, as well as geographic mobility. For example, many of the men who streamed into Denver as miners eventually switched to other occupations. Early Denverites tried out new careers frequently, just as prospectors in the hills restlessly explored new diggings.

Hundreds of individuals figured that saloonkeeping might be, as Mark Twain declared, the cheapest and easiest way to get ahead. In order to determine the validity of their hopes, career records have been compiled on all the saloonkeepers known to have been working in Denver between 1858 and 1885. Of these 1,289 individuals, evidence of employment in Denver for two or more years was located for 700 tavern owners. This smaller, more permanent group was divided into three categories on the basis of their first job as listed in the *Denver City Directory:* (1) blue-collar work, (2) saloon-keeping, and (3) white-collar work. Three hundred and forty-three individuals, or 49 percent of the total, started out as blue-collar laborers.[5] The 315 who began their Denver careers as saloonkeepers represented 45 percent of the total, while only 42, or 6 percent, started in other white-collar occupations.

As table 1 illustrates, individuals in each of these categories followed one of three possible career patterns. They either moved on to other white-collar jobs, switched to blue-collar work, or remained saloonkeepers

Table 1

Changing Occupational Status of Denver Saloonkeepers, 1858–85

Status at beginning of Denver career	Status at the end of Denver career		
	Blue-collar	Saloonkeeper	White-collar
Blue-collar 343 (49%)	45% (315)	46% (322)	9% (63)
Saloonkeeper 315 (45%)	11% (77)	63% (441)	26% (182)
White-collar 42 (6%)	4% (28)	8% (56)	88% (616)

Source: This table is based on the lives of 700 Denver saloonkeepers operating in Denver between 1858 and 1885 for whom occupational records for three or more years could be found in city directories and census manuscripts. The numbers in parentheses represent the number of individuals within the total of 700 falling into each category.

throughout their Denver careers. Tavernkeepers starting out in Denver with blue-collar jobs split about evenly between returning to blue-collar work (45 percent) and succeeding as proprietors (46 percent). A much smaller number of blue-collar beginners climbed into white-collar jobs, only 9 percent. To summarize, during their stay in Denver, a majority of blue-collar starters (55 percent) did find saloonkeeping to be a permanent step up from manual labor.[6]

Of those Denverites who began their careers as tavernkeepers, the majority remained in that occupation. This was true in 63 percent of the cases. In only 11 percent of the cases did saloonkeepers backslide to manual labor. Over a quarter of those who started as saloonkeepers (26 percent) worked their way up to more respectable white-collar positions. Again, tavernkeeping was more often than not an avenue of upward mobility.

A relatively small number of Denver's saloon men started in white-collar occupations other than saloonkeeping. Of this small group nearly all (88 percent) eventually returned to the white-collar ranks where they began. Only 8 percent remained in the bar business and only 4 percent tumbled permanently into the blue-collar realm. White-collar starters as well as saloonkeeper starters ended up in white-collar jobs twice as often as saloon-keepers who were originally blue-collar workers did.

Among the few blue-collar-origin saloonkeepers to climb securely into the white-collar world was Florian Spalti. He was born in Switzerland in 1836 and came to Colorado—the "Switzerland of America"—in 1863 as a drayman. By 1870, the census shows that Spalti had acquired a saloon and was worth twenty-five hundred dollars. Spalti's downtown saloon, where he also housed his large family, served as a headquarters from which he launched one business after another. By 1873 he conducted a grocery and a woodyard at the same address as his saloon.

"Small business but is honest and industrious," R. G. Dun and Company's agent said of Spalti two years later, adding that he owned real estate worth fifteen thousand dollars and was constructing a brick building. Spalti opened the brick structure as the Centennial Hotel in the 1880s. In the street level storefront, he continued to operate his saloon as well as a bakery, grocery, woodyard, and coal business. By 1889 the Swiss pioneer also had a real estate and insurance business. After his death in 1898, Florian Spalti was memorialized as a member of both Denver's Swiss Society and the German Turnverein and as "one of the large taxpayers of the county."[7]

Also among the 9 percent of blue-collar aspirants to reach the white-collar world was Libeus Barney, one of the gold seekers who rushed to the Pike's Peak region in 1859. Barney had been a dry-goods store clerk in New York City when he caught gold fever. Arriving in Denver, he joined the "United States of America Pike's Peak Platte River Great American Desert Gold Seekers and Diggers Company." Despite the company's impressive title, Barney's months of prospecting brought him little reward. He returned to Denver City and found another kind of pay dirt. "We purchased a lot two weeks since for $150," he wrote in July of 1859, "and are now offered for the same $500. We are putting up a building for a restaurant and concert hall which will cost some $2,000, and will pay, when completed (till spring, at least), $50 a day."[8]

Barney's Apollo Hall did pay handsomely, for it quickly became a multipurpose saloon and civic hall. The 1870 census listed the thirty-seven-year-old Barney as a "retired saloonkeeper" worth twenty-five thousand dollars and the 1873 city directory pronounced him a "capitalist." Barney's early retirement from the bar business exemplifies the exodus of the American-born from a field increasingly dominated by the foreign-born. After marrying Miss Marril E. Kendall in the First Presbyterian Church in 1872, Barney left spirit selling for a successful real estate business.

More common than the Horatio Alger success stories of Spalti and Barney were the careers of men like the O'Reilly brothers. Bernard showed up in Denver in 1871 as a laborer; he then became a miner and later a bartender. When his brother Patrick arrived in 1875, the two opened the O'Reilly Brothers Saloon. This Irish tavern did well for a quarter of a century, surviving the death of both brothers to wind up under the supervision of Katie O'Reilly. Like other proprietors of moderate means, the O'Reillys went into business by pooling the family's limited resources. Family members were a source of capital and cheap, reliable labor. The Denver city directories show that family proprietorships persisted for years while partnership saloons (another business arrangement facilitating limited-capital proprietorships) rarely lasted from one year to the next. Although depicted as enemies of family life, saloonkeepers were often married men who depended on their wives and children to help run the business.

A man's friends as well as his family were important to his bar business. Closely knit, tavern-going immigrant communities could boost one of their own into a successful liquor business. After 1870 there was a steadily increasing predominance of foreign-born saloonkeepers, as table 2 illustrates. Roughly three-fourths of the 1860 proprietors were American-born, but foreign-born proprietors had become a majority by 1870 (although less than one-fourth of the total Denver population in 1870 was foreign-born). By 1880 German-born saloonkeepers owned over a third of the Queen City's groggeries and Irish proprietors, the next largest group, owned almost one-seventh of the bars. While the Germans and Irish prevailed as saloon owners, Italians, Scandinavians, East Europeans, and Chinese made gains by 1900.

This replacement of American-born proprietors by foreign-born owners marked a major turning point in the history of the saloon. American-born whites and the population at large felt less comfortable patronizing foreign-dominated saloons and dealing with foreign-born ward bosses who oper-

Table 2
Birthplace of Denver Saloonkeepers in 1860, 1880, and 1900

Birthplace	1860	1880	1900
Canada	1	1	4
China	0	0	4
Eastern Europe and Russia	0	1	10
England and Scotland	1	6	7
France	1	4	4
Germany and Austria	7	38	86
Holland	0	0	1
Ireland	0	16	36
Italy	0	2	29
Scandinavia	0	1	27
Switzerland	1	3	8
Total Foreign-Born	11	72	216
Mid-Atlantic States	13	17	21
Midwestern States	6	9	44
New England States	4	6	9
Southern States	4	3	12
Great Plains States	1	0	7
Pacific States	0	2	1
Total Native-Born	28	37	94
Total Saloonkeepers	39	109	310

Note: The birthplace of many saloonkeepers could not be determined because of the occasional illegibility of the United States manuscript census, the source of these figures. Thus the number of saloonkeepers listed here is considerably smaller than the number known to have been operating in the last two census years treated. Because of partnerships, there were more saloonkeepers than saloons.

ated out of them. This estrangement left many taverns more vulnerable to antisaloon pressures.

Although 55 percent of the blue-collar-origin saloonkeepers succeeded in climbing into the white-collar world, another 45 percent did not. In a matter of years, months, and even weeks, these lower-class saloonkeepers slid back into the blue-collar ranks. One common path was that of the perennial bartender who eventually opened his own bar only to fail and revert to bartending for someone else. Many saloonkeepers later worked for the railroads that arrived in the 1870s or the smelters that opened in the

1880s. Other tavernkeepers, particularly among the Irish, landed jobs with the rapidly expanding municipal government as policemen or other city-service workers. Some saloonkeepers returned to the jobs they first held in the Queen City. For example, Gottlieb Koch began as a wagonmaker, then moved through a succession of jobs as a butcher, laborer, blacksmith, gardener, and, for one year, saloon proprietor, and then returned to wagonmaking. Such job changing was more common before workingmen began receiving retirement benefits in the twentieth century. Men too feeble to continue holding top-level jobs often took simpler jobs in their declining years.

Blacks who hoped to become saloonkeepers faced a difficult task, as the case of Isaac P. Brown, a mulatto laborer, illustrates. In 1871 Brown and another black opened a billiard saloon. This early black tavern did not last long; in the 1873 city directory Brown is listed as laborer. In 1875 he opened another short-lived saloon and two years later was listed as a janitor at the Denver courthouse.

In 1881, after a group of Denver blacks petitioned the city to hire blacks, Brown was sworn in as a policeman. The 1880 manuscript census shows that Brown lived in a white neighborhood, in a house with other mulattoes who, like Brown, were born in Missouri. Brown's household, reflecting the crowded housing arrangements of the poor, consisted of two married couples and two unrelated single women.

In 1886, Brown opened another saloon that survived less than a year; afterward he went back to the police force until 1890, when he became a waiter at the Gibbs House. From then until his death in 1917 he held various jobs as a waiter, farmer, and laborer. It might be concluded that the will for black capitalism was there but the established system would not yield.

Isaac Brown's thrice-suppressed career as a small-time saloonkeeper was typical of his people's fate. Out of the two dozen blacks who operated nineteenth-century Denver saloons, only three were persistent and prominent enough to attract much attention. Henry O. Wagoner, Sr., and his sister-in-law's husband, Barney L. Ford, ran notable early hostelries offering tonsorial parlors and sleeping rooms as well as food and drink. Wagoner, according to his *Denver Daily News* obituary, January 28, 1901, was a "pioneer," a friend and associate of Frederick Douglass, and "prominent in public affairs" since his 1860 arrival in Denver. With his gold-rimmed spectacles and white hair, Wagoner had been a familiar figure on the streets, "a walking encyclopedia of historical and political events of the century."

Ford's light complexion and blue eyes doubtless facilitated his successful commerce with whites. His Blake Street resort of the 1860s was a stepping stone to the fifty-three-thousand-dollar Inter-Ocean Hotel he built nearby in 1873. Although the *Rocky Mountain News* exaggerated in calling the Inter-Ocean the finest hotel in the territory, it did offer such wonders as electromagnetic annunciators (electric bells), gaslight chandeliers, and folding lace shutters in each room. The reading room contained a Brussels carpet and black-walnut desks. A grand piano and an eleven-foot-high diamond-dust mirror sparkled in the parlor, where this bright, congenial mulatto chatted with prominent white guests.

Ford and Wagoner worked together to organize Denver's blacks in a successful struggle for a black suffrage provision in the Colorado constitution and to give their tiny minority a voice in public affairs. In keeping with the rising corruption of nineteenth-century saloonhall politics, a later spokesman for Denver's black community, William Jones, was a less respected character. During his career as a Denver and Leadville saloonist, Jones's concern to protect his and other black gambling houses evidently directed his political interests. By the turn of the century, Jones was the ward boss capable of delivering Denver's black vote.[9]

While blacks considered themselves fortunate to survive in the bar business, whites often hoped to graduate from the liquor trade to bigger and better careers. About 26 percent of the Denverites who started out as saloonkeepers were able to move into more respected businesses. But a majority of the individuals who first appeared in the Queen City as saloonkeepers stuck with the bar business. Theodore Zietz, for instance, spent his entire life as a tavernkeeper, as did his son, Henry, and grandson, Henry H. Zietz, Jr.

"When my grandfather came over from Germany," Henry H. Zietz said in a 1973 interview, "he brought over this bar from his father's old tavern in Essen." Zietz caressed the massive, smooth oak bar and added, "The tables over there with the large corner racks for beer steins also came to America with my grandfather. He first set up a roadhouse in Prairie du Chien, Wisconsin, but his eight sons and seven daughters kept him so poor that he moved to Denver."[10]

Henry Zietz, Sr., moved the saloon from Market Street to a large, two-story brick structure on Osage Street in 1893. His son operated the Buckhorn on that corner until 1977, when he retired to a nursing home, heartsick at having to surrender the family business to outsiders. With some alterations, the new owners have restored and preserved the venerable Buckhorn, a unique saloon-museum of mounted animals, western artifacts, and memorabilia. Now a designated landmark, the tavern thrives along the railroad tracks in the old Auraria neighborhood and retains Colorado liquor license number one.

In contrast to saloonkeepers like Zietz, 11 percent of the early mixologists became manual laborers. Hartsville F. Jones, a Kentuckian, reached the zenith of his Denver career in the 1880s when he owned several saloons, a liquor store, and a real estate business. In 1885, while a Denver alderman, he had an elaborate crypt installed at Riverside Cemetery. In 1888 Jones ran for mayor and lost. After that his fortune took a downward turn, until his death in 1900. The 1894 directory lists him as a post office janitor and the 1896 directory shows that he was demoted to "assistant custodian." His white marble and red sandstone mausoleum remains vacant today, presumably because Jones could not keep up the payments as his circumstances worsened.[11]

When a once successful saloonkeeper like Hartsville F. Jones winds up as a menial laborer, the reason is often obscure. That alcoholism plagued Denver's saloonkeepers, however, is evident from Denver death records with their grim but common pronouncements "cirrhosis of the liver" and "chronic alcoholism."[12]

Alcoholism was an occupational hazard. It was probably a frequent factor behind the downward mobility shown by some saloonkeepers. Henry Klopper provides a tragic example. Once the owner of his own saloon, Klopper was bartending for the Jolly brothers in 1872 when the *Rocky Mountain News* reported that he was "arrested and fined Wednesday for breach of the peace, indulged in deep potations in the flowing barrel again yesterday, and afterwards tried to hang himself. He was frustrated in this design, however, and is now laboring under a fit of temporary insanity, resulting from a blow on the head, which he received several years ago, and which has been brought on by recent hard drinking."[13]

Saloon critics were not always trying to be funny when they spoke of the ardent as skull-bender, nockum stiff, pop skull, coffin varnish, and widow maker. Many alcoholics did indeed "name their own pizen."

Downward mobility for whatever reason was virtually nonexistent among the small number of Queen City saloonkeepers who started out as white-collar workers. Nearly all of these, 88 percent, eventually returned to white-collar positions other than saloonkeeping. Upper-class Denverites generally managed to remain in the respectable white-collar world. Those who toyed with the vulgar world of tavernkeeping had little trouble in eventually recovering their initial standing.

This was the case with Baron Walter von Richthofen, scion of the noted Junker family, who showed up in Denver in 1878. The bushy-bearded baron bounced from one project to another. He backed the Denver Circle Railroad that never circled the city, wrote a book on cattle raising, at which he never was successful, sold Rocky Mountain spring water as "ginger champagne," and built the elaborate Sans Souci Concert Gardens. Despite the spectacular nasturtiums, exotic imported beverages, and band, this beer garden wilted in a year or two. But the baron was of that class that could lavish thousands on a saloon, see it fail, and turn whimsically to another enterprise.

Was saloonkeeping the "cheapest" way to enter the business world? Libeus Barney built Denver's finest 1860 saloonhall for two thousand dollars But many other early grog venders dispensed spirits out of tents, wagons, the shacks they called home, or buildings that they rented cheaply. Finding the wherewithal to pay the quarterly licensing fee seems to have been a big headache for them. By 1875 Denver was collecting roughly thirty-six thousand dollars a year according to a *Rocky Mountain News* editorial:

> The city is suffering a big falling off in its revenue, owing to the decadence of the saloon business. Liquor vendors can't afford to pay $100 a quarter, and, of the thirty dealers whose licenses expire this month, nine houses notify the city clerk that they will sell no more of the ardent, at least until licenses get cheaper or times get better. Doubtless the example set by these will be followed by still others before the end of the month. While it is sad to note the falling off in the business, it is comforting to note that eighty saloons are still running, though many of them are barely able to make ends meet.[14]

The federal government also added to the financial burdens of saloon-keepers when it began collecting income taxes and annual license fees during the Civil War. Income taxes were abandoned after the war but liquor dealers, wholesale and retail, still had to take out a federal tax license.

When initially passed in 1862, the federal law taxed breweries $1 a barrel on beer, a rate lowered to 60¢ the following year. After 1865, imported liquor was assessed at 40¢ a gallon. Retail liquor licenses cost $20 a year, but many tavernkeepers had to pay additional fees for other fixtures, including a $10 annual license fee for each billiard table, $10 for a restaurant license, $100 for any theater run in conjunction with their bar, and if their saloon doubled as a hotel, from $5 to $75, depending on the size of their sleeping facilities. These federal taxes, like state and local ones, hit taverners especially hard. For example, in 1866 Barney Ford was charged $206.65 on his assessed annual income of $4,037 and $4 on his $400-piano as well as his liquor, hotel, and restaurant license fees.[15]

Saloonkeeping was a relatively easy business to enter and attracted many with limited capital and entrepreneurial experience, factors resulting in keen competition and frequent turnovers. Tavern owners organized an association in 1873 that tried to get brewers to cooperate in fixing retail beer prices at 10¢ a glass, 25¢ a quart, and $3.50 a keg.[16]

Not only intense competition from nickel-beer mongers but many other financial problems as well pursued saloonkeepers. Almost half (45 percent) of the blue-collar workers who became saloonkeepers failed to stay in the business. Tavernkeeping may have been the cheapest and easiest way to climb into the entrepreneurial world but staying there was neither cheap nor easy.

One reason that so many individuals could try the bar business was the tremendous turnover among proprietors. During the 1858–85 period, approximately half of Denver's public drinking places changed hands every year. In the earliest years an almost entirely new crew of saloonkeepers appeared annually. Satisfactory figures are not available until 1873, when the first annual city directory was published. Between 1873 and 1874 the turnover in bar proprietorship was 70.6 percent. That is to say that of the 68 saloonkeepers listed in the 1873 city directory, only 20 were still listed as saloonkeepers in 1874. By 1883–84 the turnover rate had dropped to 46.4 percent. In 1893 Denver had 433 saloonkeepers; of these, 176 were no longer in business in 1894, a turnover rate of 40.4 percent.[17]

A sample of 1873 turnover rates in a few other occupations reveals rates substantially lower than the 70 percent turnover among saloonkeepers: 51 percent for launderers, 49 percent for grocers, and 21 percent for lawyers. As was true for tavernkeepers, turnover rates among these other three occupations decreased considerably by 1893. This wide-open entreprenurial frontier, like the frontier of cheap land, was closing.

The Mile-High City's occupational turnover and the mobility of its citizens can be explained in part by its economic dependence on mining. Each new strike attracted Denverites. When silver was discovered in Leadville in the 1870s, many Denverites made the hundred-mile trip up to Colorado's magic city, whose population swelled from several hundred in the mid-1870s to almost fifteen thousand in 1880. Other discoveries in the San Juans, Aspen, Cripple Creek, and elsewhere drew upon the Mile-High City's population.

Despite the hundreds—even thousands—who left, Denver continued to grow for several reasons. For every new mineral boom, there was also an unheralded bust, resulting in a stagnant or dying mining community whose residents might return to Denver or move there for the first time. If Denver was a point of departure for the mines, it was also a point of return.

Second, Denver prospered with most new Colorado mineral discoveries because it was the financial, supply, and ore-processing center for the state. If Denverites left for the mines, newcomers poured into the city to work in its booming smelters, factories, railroads, and businesses. As mining was increasingly supplemented or replaced by less ephemeral economic activities the turnover of citizens declined.

Table 3 illustrates persistence among tavern owners during the period after 1873, when turnover for the entire city was slower than during the earlier boom-and-bust years. Even in 1873, when the town had become more stable, one-fifth of the saloonkeepers stayed in Denver only a year. At the end of five years, over half (53 percent) of the 1873 saloonkeepers had left the Queen City. Sixty-one percent of these proprietors were gone within ten years, 77 percent within twenty years, and 82 percent within thirty years. Virtually a whole new population was washed through Denver every few years by the tide of migration.

Soaring turnover rates among Denver saloonkeepers were not due only to the high in-migration and out-migration. As the lower column of table 3 demonstrates, many saloonkeepers stayed in Denver but changed occupations. Many changed jobs annually, moving restlessly into and out of

Table 3

Persistence and Average Number of Jobs Held
among Denver Saloonkeepers, 1873–85

				Number of Years					
	1	2	3	4	5	6–9	10–19	20–29	30–60
Staying in Denver	20%	9%	13%	5%	6%	14%	16%	5%	18%
Average number of jobs held	1	2	2	2	3	4	5	6	6

Source: These figures are based on a sample of the first 100 saloonkeepers (alphabetically by last name) of the total 1,289. Average number of jobs held was obtained by rounding off to the nearest whole number the average number of jobs, based on city directory listings, for each persistence group.

Table 4

Saloonkeeper Persistence by Decade, 1860–1940

First census appearance (& no. of saloonkeepers)	Saloonkeepers remaining in Denver in:									
	1860	1870	1880	1890	1900	1910	1920	1930	1940	1950
1860 (35)	35	2	0	0	0	0	0	0	0	0
1870 (48)		48	13	6	4	2	2	0	0	0
1880 (107)			107	47	24	14	5	4	1	0

Source: The number of 1860, 1870, and 1880 saloonkeepers are the same as those in table 1 (q.v.). The number of each group remaining in Denver at the end of each decade was determined by checking the city directories for 1880–1950.

the bar business. Saloonkeepers who lived in Denver two to four years averaged two different jobs during their stay in the Queen City, while five-year residents averaged three different occupations. On an average, residents of one to two decades held five different positions; and those staying for over twenty years averaged six different occupations. As might be expected, these figures indicate that population stability can be correlated with occupational stability.

Census manuscripts and city directories provide only once-a-year snapshots of a population. They do not show movement from job to job within the year. Many people switched occupation within the city-directory year, although evidence for this is not often or systematically available. Therefore, estimates of mobility in studies based on annual records, are probably underestimations. The figures in table 3 are conservative estimates; how much more frequently the population moved and changed jobs seems to be unquantifiable.

The fact that individuals moved either upward or downward on the occupational ladder is not as remarkable as the fact that they were moving constantly in both directions. As might be expected, mobility was greatest during the earliest years.[18] As table 4 illustrates, only two of the town's 1860 saloonkeepers were still in the business in 1870, and both were gone by 1880. Of the forty-eight saloonkeepers in 1870, however, over one-fourth were still peddling beer in 1880. One-eighth of the 1870 group was still around in 1890 and four of them survived into the twentieth century. Somewhat less than half the 1880 saloonkeepers were still drawing beers in 1890, over a fourth of them were still in town in 1900, and almost one-seventh of them persisted for thirty years, until 1910. Clearly, Denver's saloonkeepers were becoming more persistent as the frontier period faded.

The extensive turnover rate among Denver saloonkeepers suggests that the bar business provided the lower classes with at least one frequently used entrée into the entrepreneurial class, albeit an entrance that most nineteenth-century publicizers of "making it" in America preferred to overlook. Although almost half of the proprietorships did not survive, saloonkeeping gave a great many people of moderate means an opportunity to run their own businesses. Because the chances of success as a tavernkeeper were slightly better than even among blue-collar workers, the dream of upward mobility found considerable reinforcement in fact.

Chapter 6
THE IMMIGRANT SALOON

For the Queen City's European immigrants, the saloon represented more than an economic opportunity. In their struggle to establish roots in a new country, many of them relied on taverns as both a haven for Old World culture and an introduction to their new home.

While some Denverites attacked the saloon as a nest of inferior peoples, political corruption, and moral debasement, many foreign-born newcomers felt differently. They relished their taverns as clubs and community centers for a wide range of social, political, and economic functions, just as the first Denverites depended on the multifunctional frontier saloon.

Throughout the nineteenth century, the foreign-born constituted roughly a fourth of Denver's population. Nearly all of these foreigners came from beer-, whiskey-, or wine-drinking cultures. Over 80 percent came from Germany, Ireland, Scandinavia, England, Canada, Scotland, China, Italy, and the Slavic countries, in that order.[1] Mexicans did not come to Denver in large numbers until the twentieth century and did not become the city's largest ethnic group until after World War II.

Germans were Denver's most prominent, prosperous, and populous immigrant group, with homes and taverns scattered throughout the city. By 1880 over one-third of all Denver's saloons were owned by Germans. Inside these taverns, customers spoke and sang in German, read German newspapers and magazines, consumed sauerkraut and strudel, and quaffed German beer and wine. Establishments such as the Edelweiss, Turner Hall, Bavarian House, Kaiserhof, Deutsches House, Germania Hall, Mozart Hall, Saxonia Hall, Heidelberg Cafe, and Walhalla Hall offered not only "Dutch [Deutsch, or German] lunches" but the customs and culture of the Old Country as well.

Turner Hall, the best known of the German taverns, was founded in 1865–66, and continues to house the oldest continually operating ethnic club in Colorado. The club's origins can be traced to the Turnverein, a society organized in Prussia around 1811 to promote German nationalism and gymnastic exercise. Initially the Denver membership met in Adolph Schinner's City Bakery and Saloon; but they moved into successively larger quarters, finally settling in the fine four-story turreted hall erected on Arapahoe Street in 1889. Besides a drinking hall, the Turnverein had exercise rooms equipped by Denver's various German-owned breweries. At the urging of the German community, exercise classes were also inaugurated in the Denver public schools after the Turnverein donated the salary for the first physical education instructor.

By 1880 Turner Hall, or the "German Temple of Art," as historian William B. Vickers called it, was the most commodious hall in Denver. It housed not only German community affairs but also public concerts, plays, operas, lectures, and political rallies. Turner Hall also served as a chapel for funerals. Traditionally members planned in advance to treat their funeral parties to lunch and beer at the hall.[2]

An 1874 incident at Turner Hall demonstrated the political influence of the Germans, an influence that protected them while other foreigners were subjected to varying degrees of discrimination. When a Denver policeman attempted to arrest a patron for after-hours drinking, the Germans ejected the officer and notified city hall, "We want it clearly understood that we want no policeman in our hall in any official capacity." In deference to the powerful Teutonic community, Mayor Francis Case sent an apologetic letter promising to ignore the midnight closing law at Turner Hall.[3]

Germans, including many in the liquor business, quickly became entrenched in the Queen City's aristocracy. One-time saloonkeepers John J. Reithman and his brother-in-law, John Milheim, and the brewers John Good, Philip Zang, and Adolph Coors made enough money to place themselves in the upper circles of the elite. Many prominent Germans enhanced their countrymen's fortunes in Denver. Frederick Steinhauer, a founder of the Turnverein and a member of the territorial legislature, wrote to German newspapers in Germany extolling Colorado as "a better place for a young man to secure his living and independence." As a member of the Denver school board, Steinhauer promoted German language and culture and donated German primers to schools.[4]

Many Denverites benefited from the German interest in music and the arts. In 1873, the saloonkeeping Kaltenbach family ordered a ten-thousand-dollar orchestrion from Berlin. When the elaborate organ arrived a year later the Kaltenbachs renamed their tavern Orchestrion Hall. It took a week to assemble and tune the massive, eleven-foot-high machine and attach the reeds, horns, drums, and xylophone. To celebrate the instrument's premiere, hundreds crowded into the hall. "No one," an observer recalled, "had ever supposed there were so many Germans in the region and [all] were amazed that the beer held out through the long night." As Germans drank their brew and sang along, the largest musical apparatus between the Missouri River towns and California ground out "Die Wacht am Rhein," Robert Schumann's "Traumerei," George Schweitzer's "Yodel Hi Lee Hi Loo," and Ludwig van Beethoven's "Moonlight Sonata."[5]

Germans gave the young city music and culture and one of its first festivals, Bock Beer Day. This traditional German holiday came in the spring, when brewers cleaned out their fermenting vats and made from the residue a syrupy brew called bock beer. The *Rocky Mountain News* for May 21, 1874, reported that all nationalities joined in the beer fest as large wagons from the local breweries, decorated with flags and laden with kegs of beer, rumbled continuously through the streets to the saloons. Otto Heinrich's at Sixteenth and Larimer streets set the record for Bock Beer Day, 1874, serving some 3,000 glasses of beer, 50 loaves of bread, and 125 pounds of meat.

Germans led happier lives in nineteenth-century Denver than many other ethnic groups, but two important events of the early twentieth century changed the situation. Because their wealth was heavily invested in the liquor business, Germans came under attack from Prohibitionists. Countering the attacks of the "temperentzlers," Germans met at the Turner Hall to organize the Citizens Protective Union, which defended the saloon as "the poor man's club house, his restaurant, and his infirmary."[6]

When Coloradans voted to inaugurate statewide prohibition in 1916, many Germans lost their jobs in the liquor industry. The Zang Brewery, Neef Brothers Brewery, and dozens of other manufacturers, wholesalers, and distributors closed along with over four hundred Denver saloons. Many more Germans were affected by the tavern closings because beerhalls had traditionally served as social centers. An even heavier blow to the Teutonic community came with the outbreak of World War I. Germans became the target of a widespread and irrational hate campaign. Regardless of their professed and proven patriotism, German Americans were fired from their jobs, illegally imprisoned, and physically and verbally abused. Denver public schools outlawed German language classes and restaurants began calling sauerkraut "liberty cabbage" and hamburgers "liberty steaks."[7] After the double-barreled blow of prohibition and World War I, this group that contributed much to Denver's cultural, social, and saloon life never fully reemerged as a distinctive ethnic group. Simultaneously, the once ubiquitous German saloon largely vanished from the Denver cityscape.

Denver's Irish, like the Germans, usually melted into the city's nineteenth-century mainstream. "No Irish Need Apply" signs stayed back on the eastern seaboard for several reasons. The presence of Indians, Orientals, and blacks in western cities tended to push the English-speaking, white-skinned Irish up the social ladder a few notches. If people could assert their superiority over red, yellow, and black men, they were less inclined to discriminate against fellow whites.

Irishmen were also well received in Denver because those who traveled this far west usually had some money or guaranteed jobs with the railroads, smelters, or other businesses. By the time they reached Denver, typical "children of Erin" often had lived in other North American cities, where they had learned to speak understandable English and acquired job skills.

Indeed, Irish laborers were welcome in rapidly industrializing and labor-short Denver, as a letter reprinted in the *Rocky Mountain News* suggested: "Dear Patrick come! A dollar a day for ditching, no hanging for staling, Irish petaties a dollar a bushel, and Whiskey the same! Dear Patrick come, If you can't come in one vessel, come in two."[8]

Many came as "terriers," as the Irish railroad crews called themselves. Irishmen moved into trackside, working-class neighborhoods in Auraria, north Denver, and north-central Denver. Soon after their arrival, some of them established blue-collar bars strategically located between the jobs and homes of their countrymen. Passersby reported barroom fights between Irish Catholics and Irish Orangemen and that alcoholic aromas and the lyrics of "My Wild Irish Rose," "You'll Never Find a Coward Where Shamrock Grows," "Wearin' of the Green," and "Where the River Shannon Flows" drifted out of open pub doors. Of all the immigrant groups, the Emerald Islanders seemed to be the most addicted to saloons, heavy drinking, and alcoholism.

Saloons promoted Irish clubs and helped distribute the *Rocky Mountain Celt,* which claimed to be the only Irish-American newspaper in the West. Denver chapters of the Ancient Order of Hibernians, the Irish Progressive Society, the Irish Fellowship Association, the Irish Land League, and the St. Patrick's Mutual Benevolent Society were established by the 1880s. Saloonkeeper Patrick Frain spearheaded the Land League's fund-raising for Irish independence, while the Benevolent Society sought to encourage Gaelic literature, lectures, and band music. While some of these groups convened in bars, one Irish organization, St. Joseph's Catholic Total Abstinence Society, attempted to dry out the city's hard-drinking Emerald Islanders. The abstainers found a president and benefactor in Denver's foremost Irish industrialist, miller John K. Mullen.

Irishmen united in 1881 to elect the city's first Irish-born mayor, Robert Morris. He came to Denver in the 1870s as a land agent for the Kansas Pacific Railroad, subsequently opened a men's furnishing store and other businesses, and also found time to build up a following among the members of the Land League over which he presided. His election, as John K. Mullen noted, "united the Irishmen as they have never been united before." Although 80 percent of Denver's Irish registered as Democrats, they crossed party lines en masse to give their Republican countryman a three-hundred-vote victory over a German hardware storeman, George Tritch.[9]

Irish solidarity and saloonhall shenanigans reached an annual climax on March 17. Initially the Ancient Order of Hibernians conducted drinking-and-dancing festivals in honor of St. Patrick; and in the 1890s a coalition of clubs, churches, and taverns began sponsoring a downtown parade of celebrants bedecked with green ribbons. Mayor Robert W. Speer pronounced the parade an official city celebration in 1906. A decade later, the festival fizzled after the inauguration of prohibition. And when Ireland, or at least the Irish Republican Army, began flirting with Germany during World War I, Denverites dropped the parade entirely. Anti-Catholic, antiimmigrant, pro–Ku Klux Klan sentiment during the 1920s further discouraged would-be celebrants of St. Patrick's Day. Not until 1962 did a group of Denver Irishmen, convening in Duffy's Shamrock Tavern, launch a successful campaign to reinstate the parade in honor of Ireland's patron saint.

Although the Irish-born represented less than 3 percent of the Mile-High City's population in 1900, they operated 10 percent of the city's taverns. This statistic helps to explain why Irishmen were able, in a predominantly non-Irish city, to elect Irish mayors and councilmen. For the group's political power revolved around an alliance of saloonkeepers, politicians, and policemen, three occupational groups that attracted large numbers of gregarious, politically sensitive Irishmen.

Among many Irish clans, at least one policemen, one politician, and one saloonkeeper could be found. Policemen, whether Irish or not, commonly had saloon connections. Early-day police chiefs David J. Cook and James B. Veatch were one-time saloonkeepers, as were detective Sam Howe and marshal "Noisy Tom" Pollock. Cornelius J. ("Coney the Fox") Kelleher, operator of one of the most notorious gambling saloons, began his Denver career as a deputy sheriff. Andrew Horan served, at one time or another, as a saloonkeeper, a policeman, and a city councilman. Denver, like many other American cities, has a roster of mayors and council members that bristles with Irish names to this day.

Of Denver's pub-keeping aldermen, one of the most successful was Eugene Madden, a second-generation Irishman. He served nine consecutive city council terms between 1912 and 1941 with strong support from his Larimer Street saloon and the nearby police department, where his brother was a captain. Constituents could call councilman Madden anytime, day or night, to get a friend or relative into a job or out of jail. He was a soft-spoken man who walked his Auraria ward, giving kisses to the babies, candy to the ladies, and food and coal to the needy. If he bailed out Saturday-night troublemakers, he also offered Sunday-morning support to the neighborhood's Irish church, St. Leo's. Successful as both a councilman and a tavern owner, Madden was one preprohibition saloonkeeper to survive the seventeen-year drought and reopen in 1933.[10]

Irishmen found politics to be good business. Irish-born brothers Michael and John Flaherty, for instance, came to Denver around 1890 to work at the Globe Smelter. After years of smelter toil, they opened Flaherty's Saloon on Larimer Street. When prohibition closed the bar, Michael switched to the construction business, where his support of Mayor Robert

W. Speer paid off. But although political connections helped Flaherty earn initial contracts to do city streets, alleys, and sewers, it was his fine work (he even used glazed bricks in sewers) and pride in living up to his contracts that enabled him to stay in business.[11]

Although Irish saloonkeeping politicians were stereotyped as corrupt and intemperate, this was not necessarily the case. Even the Voters' League, a reform group hostile to saloons, found that at least one Irish tavern "has always been considered a model institution and was never known to be a scene of drunkenness or grafting." Thomas Henry, the Irish-born owner of this Market Street bar, never drank to excess nor drank at all while tending bar, according to the League's character assessment in 1904, when he ran for district supervisor.[12]

If some Irishmen found their saloons to be bases for political, police, and business life, many others found taverns a congenial place to gather. Dull but exhausting jobs led them to bars. Their culture and even their church sanctioned drink. The saloon, declared Father Thomas Malone, editor of the *Colorado Catholic,* was the "working man's club."[13]

Denver's Jewish population, like other nineteenth-century groups, found the liquor business relatively easy to enter. Frederick Zadek Salomon opened one of Denver's first general stores selling, among other things, ale from Denver's Rocky Mountain Brewery, which he cofounded with Charles Tascher. Salomon became active in Denver's first Board of Trade in the 1860s and also helped organize the Hebrew Burial and Prayer Society in 1860. Charles M. Schayer, who started out with a small liquor and cigar store in 1870 and became one of Denver's larger wholesale liquor dealers, was a German Jew. He served as a founder, first treasurer, and second president of Temple Emanuel, the Queen City's first synagogue. Samuel Rose, N. Rosenthal, Joseph Bloch, Benjamin Hamburger, and Moses Sporberg, all liquor dealers at one time or another, were also among the twenty-four Jews who organized the pioneer synagogue.[14]

Jews did not suffer the violent and intensive discrimination that blacks, Orientals, and (to a lesser extent) Italians did. They held prominent commercial, professional, and political positions that gave their people economic and political clout. "The Hebrews of Denver," declared the September 1, 1881 *Denver Times,* upon completion of Temple Emanuel at Twenty-fourth and Curtis streets, "are to be congratulated and complimented upon having so fine a synagogue and upon the high grade of social and intellectual standing of the members."

Yet discrimination against the Jews existed, as the confidential reports of R. G. Dun's Denver agent in 1871 and 1874 indicate. In assessing the character of Samuel Rose, a founder, president, and major supporter of Temple Emanuel, the Denver agent belabored the fact that he was a Jew. While admitting that Rose's liquor and cigar business did well and enjoyed good credit locally, the Dun appraiser told the New York office that he was "not of good character and standing. Too quarrelsome and revengeful. Whips his wife . . . a Jew." A later report asserted, "[Rose's] trade is primarily with the small class of saloon men and he necessarily takes large risks. He does too large a credit business for his capital."[15]

Upper-class and commercial discrimination against the Jews emerged with the development of exclusive clubs in the 1880s. The Denver Club began in the 1860s as the Denver Whist and Chess Club, of which Frederick Salomon was a founder and tavernkeeper Isadore Deitsch a director. Yet in 1881, when the whist and chess players reorganized as the Denver Club—the city's most influential club—Jews were barred from membership. Consequently, they formed their own town and country clubs, which flourish to this day.

Denver's early Jews, who came primarily from German backgrounds, frequently did well in spite of occasional anti-Semitism and the resulting business handicaps. The election of merchant Wolfe Londoner, a Jew, as mayor in 1889 symbolized their general acceptance into the community. "I was surprized by the prominent number of Hebrew politicians," reported an 1877 visitor, Rabbi Isaac Mayer Wise, who estimated that there were only five hundred Jews in the entire state.[16]

This situation began to change, however, in the 1890s. Hundreds of Jewish families from Russia and Eastern Europe settled in Colorado. Many of them were unskilled; few spoke English. They worked as peddlers, box makers, junk dealers, day laborers, ragpickers, and bottle pickers. They became the bogeymen of Denver, strange-looking and strange-talking people who were teased, taunted, and molested as they scoured city streets and alleys for recyclable refuse, rags, and bottles. One Jewish ragpicker was attacked by what the *Jewish Outlook* called "Christian hoodlums." He was insulted and beaten; and his rickety wagon, with its load of rags, was burned. Another child of the Jewish ghetto along West Colfax Avenue recalled that he and his family dressed in gunny sacks to soften the stonings that his people received. This fellow's father, a schochet (a butcher of animals for use as food in Jewish households) at a slaughterhouse, was forced to bring beer to work for the gentile employees. If they did not get their beer, they told him, he would not get his work.[17]

Despite some persecution, the Jewish newcomers maintained their religion, their identity, and their culture, partly with the aid of several Jewish tavernkeepers. One of their first sources of kosher food was Albert Wongrowitz's popular saloon and delicatessen, located next to Temple Emanuel. Patrons lingered beside "Wongy's" warm stove to hear the community's history, gossip, and news while they enjoyed lox, bagels, and wine. Adolph Goldhammer opened his West Side Family Liquor House to the Hebrew community for meetings, debates, lectures, and plays. Other Jewish immigrants also operated delicatessens that were second only to the synagogues as preservers of Jewish customs.

In comparison with most German, Irish, and Jewish immigrants, Italians got a chilly reception in the Queen City of the Plains. Only a sprinkling of Italians settled in Denver before 1880, when the census taker found 86 natives of Italy. In the following decade, however, the railroads and other industrial operations recruited cheap Italian labor; and by 1890 Denver had 608 Italians. Despite economic and cultural obstacles, they slowly progressed from the lower ranks of society and their homes in the Platte River bottoms. A few respectable Italian tavernkeepers played a major role in the emergence of their countrymen, while several disreputable Italian bars and barroom murders damaged their standing in the city.

In the summer of 1872, Angelo Capelli settled in Denver, where he opened a small produce stand and, soon afterward, the Highland House. Capelli's career demonstrated that geographic mobility on the frontier could bring success. He had failed in St. Louis and opened his Denver business under his wife's name, a dodge that did not escape the attention of Denver credit agents. Despite his limited capital and poor credit appraisal, this early Italian innkeeper did well. Two years later the Capellis owned several properties, could get credit for "any reasonable amount," and were worth about five thousand to six thousand dollars clear. Presumably because of the favorable reports that Angelo and his wife sent home about the thriving city of the 1870s, other Capellis began trickling into Denver. They operated several family taverns and by 1890 also had opened a confectionery shop, a macaroni factory, a meat market, fruit stands, and a real estate business. To assist the growing number of Italian immigrants to Colorado, Capelli was appointed in 1880 as Denver's first Italian consul.[18]

Peter Albi, another early saloonkeeper, housed the Italian Publishing Company and the Italian gazette *Roma* in his Fifteenth Street tavern. He and his family took up the grocery business in 1891, banking in 1892, and real estate and the Cascade Laundry Company in the 1920s. Albi sponsored roughly one hundred Italian immigrants to Denver, promising immigration authorities that he would find homes and jobs for his Calabrian countrymen.[19] Other leading Italian families—the Aiellos, the Carbones, the Frazzinis, the Mosconis, and the Zarlengos—also established inns that served their growing community.

A few Italians established successful nineteenth-century businesses, but the majority found only the poorest of jobs, primarily as day laborers. Hundreds lived in river-bottom shacks and tents. Along the South Platte, at least, their children could gather watercress to sell in the city market. And the river provided these former European peasants with water for their vegetable patches. Many of them hawked their produce in carts on Larimer Street. As the Queen City grew and their gardens flourished, many of these riverside farmers acquired enough capital to buy horses and wagons. After putting canvas roofs on the wagons and hanging scales on the sides, Italians peddled their produce in Denver neighborhoods and suburbs, calling out, "Vegetable man! Vegetable man! Nice-a-ripa-tomatoes."

Some street peddlers saved enough to establish less peripatetic businesses. Tony Zarlengo began his new life in Denver as a day laborer in 1898, switched to peddling two years later, and in another two years converted his first residence, at 1905 Division Street under the Twentieth Street viaduct, into a saloon. Other one-time street vendors developed Denver's huge wholesale produce plants, which still flourish along the Platte bottomlands where Italians first found fertile soil.

Initially impoverished, illiterate, and unskilled, the Italian immigrants were disliked by some Denver nativists for their inability to speak English, their Catholicism, their eating and drinking habits, and their occasional criminality. The prejudices of Denverites were inflamed by the bizarre events of October 1875, which came to be called the Italian murders. These grisly deeds came to light when countless flies swarming around the windows and the ever increasing stench from an abandoned shack on Lawrence Street prompted authorities to investigate. A trapdoor in the kitchen led to the basement where four bloody bodies were found, their throats slashed from ear to ear. As newspapers headlines announced, the dead were Italians and so were their murderers.

The memory of that crime was still vivid eighteen years later when Denver barkeeper Daniel Arata murdered an elderly, indigent Civil War veteran unable to pay for his nickel beer. A mob of hundreds, according to the *Denver Republican* for July 27, 1893, tore up streetcar tracks to use as battering rams. After poking a hole in the wall of the county jail, they broke through a steel door to get to Arata, whom they dragged to a noose dangling from a tree in the jail yard. An army of latecomers arrived and, disappointed that they missed the lynching, decided to do it again. The corpse was rehanged at Seventeenth and Champa streets as men with distorted faces yelled, "Arata killed an old soldier for a nickel" and "Death to the Dago."[20]

Another murder in an Italian saloon aroused the Queen City's prejudices in 1901. Frank Lotito was shot after a barroom row, evidently caused by the rivalry between more prosperous northern Italians and poorer southern Italians from violent black-hand societies. Newspaper stories also denounced Denver's numerous Italian saloons as havens for merchandising stolen property.

The Capellis, the Albis, and other respectable Italian families were concerned about the impoverished and violent elements of their community. Partly in the hope of Americanizing and refining their poorer countrymen, they established Columbus Hall and the Italian-American Club. Siro Mangini, who married one of the Capelli daughters, named his Larimer Street tavern after Christopher Columbus. Surely, Mangini thought, here was one Italian whom Americans knew and appreciated. At Christopher

Columbus Hall, Mangini dished out free ravioli to neighboring shopkeepers, politicians, and policemen who walked the beat. Mrs. Mangini and their ten children, who lived above the saloon, worked all day to prepare these monthly feasts. Because of the Manginis' efforts, Italians found themselves more welcome, at least on Larimer Street.[21]

Mangini and fellow tavernkeepers Luigi Mosconi and Joseph Turre formed the Unione Fratellanza and Augustine Roncagalia, proprietor of the Columbia House, introduced the Garibaldi Society to Denver. Michael Notary, coowner of the North Denver Liquor House, founded the Mount Carmel Society. Frank Mazza, another successful businessman who started out as a tavern owner, helped found Unione e Fratellanza Italiana, Bersaglieri Principedi Napoli, and the Club Italo Americano. The Societa Nativi de Potenza, founded in 1899, still survives with the continuing support of tavernkeeping clans such as the Smaldones and Aiellos. These ethnic clubs played a role in helping the Italians to succeed. Leaving behind their tents and shacks in the bottomlands, Italians moved up into the elegant, tree-shaded neighborhoods of north Denver and Highlands. Here they opened up some of the more elegant and popular restaurants and bars of twentieth-century Denver.

Unlike some native-born Americans but like many other Europeans, Italians regarded wine and spirits as a healthy, basic ingredient of their culture. Denver's Italian Catholic church, Our Lady of Mount Carmel, fully sanctioned this drinking tradition. The church's outspoken first pastor, Father Mariano Felice Lepore, even became the well-known advocate of one would-be saloon. When Paulo DeJeune encountered neighborhood and city opposition to opening a saloon near a north Denver Catholic school in 1901, Father Lepore vigorously but unsuccessfully argued that the tavern be built.[22]

When prohibition came, Italian abstinence did not. Italians resorted to the basements of their homes or the backrooms of taverns that had been converted to soft-drink parlors, where they made, aged, and drank their own wine. Soon Italians supplied spirits to thousands of other thirsty Denverites as well, through speakeasies and bootlegging operations. Regardless of what the law said, the tavern and the glass of wine were too essential to the Italian lifestyle to be abandoned.

Thousands of Slavic immigrants from Eastern Europe, hoping to escape the poverty, wars, and political chaos of the Austro-Hungarian and Russian empires, came to Colorado between 1880 and World War I. By 1900 they constituted the fourth largest foreign-born group in the Queen City. They included Slovaks, Slovenians, Serbs, Croats, Poles, and Russians. By 1920, the Russians had become the single largest group immigrating to Colorado (census figures do not distinguish Slavic Russians from non-Slavic Russian Jews and Germans from Russia), with Yugoslavs,

Czechoslovakians, and Poles the twelfth, thirteenth, and fourteenth largest groups, respectively.[23]

Slavs tended to settle along the South Platte River just north of Denver, near the smelters where many of them worked. The town of Globeville, named for a leading smelter, had a predominantly Slavic population, with some Germans from Russia, Scandinavians, Italians, and others. It was among the most impoverished settlements in the Denver area, as the Slavs soon discovered. Smelter smoke and stockyard stench hovered about their homes. Streets remained unpaved and sidewalks were nonexistent long after Denver annexed the town in 1902. Globeville became home not only for poor immigrants, the smelters, and the stockyards, but also for the rail yards of the Union Pacific and Burlington railroads. Denver's Riverside Cemetery was located in the area in 1876, followed by the municipal poorhouse in the 1880s. Meatpacking and rendering plants, iron works, and the city's asphalt plant were also located there. Later, an early public-housing project and interstate highways carved up the Globeville neighborhood.

Life in Globeville was hard. Slavic newcomers gathered old boxcar lumber from the railroad repair shops and reused old nails to build their homes. Slavic families landscaped their yards with vegetable patches, chicken houses, pigpens, and rabbit hutches. Often children added to the menagerie and family menus when they visited the stockyards, where railroad unloaders gave away calves, piglets, and lambs born in transit. To help feed their families, youngsters slipped under parked railroad grain cars and drilled holes in the floors to fill burlap bags with wheat and corn for empty cupboards at home.[24]

Some of the smelter companies constructed housing for their employees. Typical of company housing was Sheedy Row, an alley of homes between Washington Street and the Globe Smelter. The row of shacks was named for Dennis Sheedy, president of the Globe Smelting and Refining Company. With the profits he made by underpaying and underhousing smelter workers, Sheedy built his mansion at 1115 Grant Street, the "millionaires' row" of Capitol Hill, several miles to the south of Sheedy Row and many more miles away socially.

At the turn of the century, the American Smelting and Refining Company's Globe and Grant plants paid common laborers a minimum wage of $1.75 for a ten-hour day and skilled smelter workers between $2.50 and $3.50 per twelve-hour day.[25] Some of these workingmen found inexpensive housing in Globeville's numerous saloons, which usually contained a first-floor bar and second-story sleeping rooms. The Globe Hotel, for instance, was a smelter-owned store, boarding house, and tavern across the street from the Globe smelter. Although prices were high, the company did extend credit because paychecks were delivered through the hotel, which could take out housing, grocery, and bar bills. After these deductions, the workingman often went home on payday with only a few dollars in his pocket for a month's work.

Miserable working conditions whetted laborers' appetites for barroom relaxation. Teamster Joe Tekavec recalled Joseph Prijatau's Saloon: "We'd water our mules at the big trough outside and then go in and water ourselves. You could get a big mug of beer for five cents and then there was free lunch fixings on the end of the bar, too. Prijatau's was a big, two-story place with smelter workers staying upstairs. When the 3:00 P.M. whistle blew over at the Globe Smelter they'd come out of Prijatau's Saloon like bees out of a hive." Globeville's bars also had take-out service. "They'd fill up a five-pound lard can with suds," Tekavec reminisced, "for only a dime." Washington Street (which was called Watervliet Avenue until about 1904) was the main street of Globeville and was lined with about a dozen saloons at the turn of the century. Among the more notable were the Smelters' Exchange Saloon and the Smeltermen's No. 93 Saloon, which advertised, "Foreign languages interpreted."[26]

Globeville's many Slavic saloons also served as the neighborhood's community centers. John Predovich's hall at 4837 Washington Street housed religious, fraternal, and union groups. Meetings to establish Holy Rosary Slovenian Catholic Church and meetings of St. Martin's Polish National Alliance and the smelter workers took place at Predovich's. Activities of the Czech-Slavic Benefit Society were conducted in the saloon of Vaclav Cerney, who served as the group's chairman. Globeville politics centered on the so-called king of the Slavs, Max Malich, who reigned from his popular saloon.[27] Malich, who spoke four languages, was a political broker who could deliver the votes. Walter Root's saloon and boarding-house became the Western Slavonic Association Hall after the group's incorporation in 1908. In this alliance of various Slavic groups, the poor immigrants of Globeville pooled their capital to help each other overcome hardships. The association still provides members with life and home insurance, sends flowers to the sick, and arranges funerals.

In poor communities like Globeville, saloons functioned as banks. The business manager for the American Smelting and Refining Company, which controlled Denver's smelters by 1900, complained to the Colorado Board of Labor Arbitration: "Fifty per cent of the checks paid to our employees for years back have been cashed by saloon-men, and the canceled checks show it. Over $2,500,000 of the concern's money has been laid out over saloon bars, amid the fumes of whiskey and beer."[28] In Globeville, saloons, not banks, were held up. Thieves made off with $140 in cash and four smelter checks in an 1887 holdup at the St. Louis Beer Hall.[29]

The Slavs have been slow to abandon their old neighborhood and its taverns. The Slovenian Home, Western Slavonic Association, St. Jakob's Croatian-Slovenian Club, and St. Martin's Society of the Polish National

Alliance still exist. John Popovich's Slovenian Gardens still serves as a social center for Slavic Globeville, although in 1977 Popovich lamented, "We're the last survivor of all those old Slavic saloons."[30]

Among the social institutions that European immigrants valued, saloons were the most conspicuous and numerous. Nativists condemned these bars as impediments to Americanizing newcomers and centers where Old World values were perpetuated. Indeed, prohibition was, in part, an effort to eliminate these havens of "inferior" peoples, an effort by white Protestant Americans to discipline predominantly Catholic and Jewish immigrants. "The foreign population," as one national prohibition leader phrased a standard argument, "is largely under the social and political control of the saloon."[31]

Reformers argued that, in order to Americanize immigrants and curb their political power, the saloon must be abolished. Nativist opposition to the saloon was strong in Denver, which had fewer foreign-born citizens than most large cities—only 23 percent of the population in 1890. As many as ten thousand Denverites joined the anti-immigrant, anti-Catholic American Protective Association (A.P.A.) by 1894. Although the A.P.A. all but disappeared a few years later, nativism did not, as the popularity of the Ku Klux Klan in the 1920s demonstrated. Colorado's per capita Klan membership was second only to Indiana's hooded empire, and Denver proved to be one of the more insular and xenophobic American cities.[32]

Branded as un-American, foreign-born pubkeepers draped their resorts with American flags, hung portraits of American presidents, generals, and heroes, and displayed replicas of Abraham Lincoln's saloon license. In the late 1890s they "remembered the Maine" conspicuously and even turned their taverns into recruiting stations for the Spanish-American War. Yet nothing, not even giving their lives in war, would prove their patriotism to some Americans.

Prohibitionists and nativists agreed that saloons functioned as bastions of cultural diversity and multipurpose immigrant centers. Poor immigrants cashed their checks, sought loans, and deposited money with saloonkeepers. Saloons dispensed foreign-language literature and some tavernkeepers read and wrote letters for their illiterate customers. In poorer neighborhoods, saloons might be the only place where people could simply sit down for a rest, get a glass of water, use the toilet, or wash themselves. Saloons were also orientation centers for newcomers. Politically, the saloon harbored both front-hall rallies and back-room deals. Xenophobic Americans complained that they were havens for un-American activities. The multifunctional immigrant saloon drew the combined attacks of nativists worried about swelling foreign populations, of progressives concerned about the city's saloon-infested slums, and of prohibitionists who tended to blame all social problems on alcohol. Forgetting that Denver's predominantly American-born pioneers had relied on the saloon for many uses, second-generation Denverites condemned the tavern as a detrimental foreign institution.

In their effort to eliminate immigrant saloons, nativists and prohibitionists were largely successful. When repeal came in 1933, few immigrant bars reappeared. With the exception of a proliferation of Mexican bars, these bastions of Denver's foreign-born communities largely vanished. "Last night," a voluptuous blonde sang in the Heidelberg Cafe in the early-morning hours of January 1, 1916, "was the end of the world."[33] The song was prophetic for hundreds of immigrant saloons. During the decades following prohibition, the Kaiserhof became the Kenmark and the Edelweiss was transformed into Keables Sandwich Shop. Walhalla Hall became a Walgreen Drug Store. Goldhammer's Yiddish tavern in west Denver's Little Jerusalem reemerged nondenominational and nondescript as Jim and Freida's Bar. Siro Mangini's Christopher Columbus Hall became the El Bronco Bar and Aiello's Italian Village was rechristened Patsy's Inn. Madden's Saloon, the long-time center of Irish political power and social life, was replaced by Al's Super Service Station. John Predovich's saloon, the one-time stronghold of Globeville's Slavic community activity, reemerged in the post-prohibition era as the Mayflower Bar.

Chapter 7
MORAL GEOGRAPHY

For every foreign-born immigrant moving to nineteenth-century Denver, three Americans settled in the burgeoning Rocky Mountain metropolis. By 1890, Denver had become the third largest western city (after San Francisco and Omaha) and the twenty-fifth largest in the United States. The frontier town was only a memory by 1890, when Denver's population density surpassed that of Washington, Kansas City, Minneapolis, St. Paul, or Omaha. Denver had come to resemble the large industrial cities of the East more than a western frontier town.[1]

Not only the size but also the nature of the population changed. Trappers, traders, miners, cowboys, farmers, and other frontier types were supplanted by blue-collar workers and business and professional people. In the rough frontier town of 1860, men outnumbered women seven to one; but forty years later females held a slight majority, and Denver was far more genteel.

A writer for *Harper's Magazine* found the Denver of the 1890s filled with "New Yorkers, Bostonians, Philadelphians, and New Orleans men. Englishmen—the well-to-do and well-brought-up from all over the country." Most of them came not to find wealth but to nurse their health (Colorado's dry climate was widely prescribed as a cure for tuberculosis, asthma, and other lung diseases). Frequently these newcomers devoted themselves to urban reform and cultural, educational, philanthropic, and religious activities. "On its worst side," the *Harper's* correspondent added, "the city is western, and its moral side is eastern."[2]

Whether eastern, western, or both, this moral element saw Denver's numerous saloons as useless, even dangerous vestiges of the frontier period. Overlooking the merits of the multifunctional pioneer and immigrant saloons, they formed or reinforced local chapters of the Anti-Saloon League, the Woman's Christian Temperance Union, the Prohibition party, and other dry organizations. Many of them moved into saloonless streetcar suburbs and fought to keep them that way. They launched a campaign to confine saloons to previously existing urban sites; and even there, prohibitionists did all they could to make the saloonkeeper's survival difficult, a phenomenon that one scholar has called moral geography.[3]

Railroads were the main force behind the population growth and social change that fostered moral geography. Before the iron tracks reached Denver in 1870, the self-proclaimed city was actually a stagnating town. Between 1860 and 1870, the community at the confluence gained only ten residents, according to the federal census taker. The city acquired a dozen railroads between 1870 and 1880, however, and the population increased by seven times, from 4,759 to 35,629. Although the dispossession of the Indians, improved mining techniques, and the silver boom also promoted growth, the railroads were primarily responsible for revitalizing the busted boom town.

The town, initially strung out along the South Platte River and Cherry Creek, began stretching out along the Denver Pacific (later Union Pacific) tracks to the north and the Denver and Rio Grande and Denver, South Park and Pacific lines to the south. By the 1880s the city had spread northward to its current boundary of Fifty-second Avenue and the company towns that arose around the Argo, Globe, and Swansea smelters. South Denver, also a trackside community, became the southern boundary suburb by the end of the 1880s.

Auraria, the oldest neighborhood in the city, had declined during the 1860s after many businesses moved across Cherry Creek to be near the stage depot. With the arrival of the railroad, however, Auraria boomed again. The Denver and Rio Grande, the Denver, South Park and Pacific, and later the Colorado and Southern railroads built facilities in Auraria, transforming the area into a thriving center for railroad men. Hundreds of plants, shops, and homes went up and some of the old Ferry Street saloons returned to life. Auraria also began attracting trackside industry, including an ore-sampling plant, the Tivoli Brewery, and several flour mills, including that of John Kernan Mullen, whose Hungarian Flour Mill eventually became one of the largest in the West. As industry, commerce, and homes spread south and west along the tracks, the working-class Auraria neighborhood over-flowed southward.

Across Cherry Creek, in old Denver City, the railroads also spatially and economically restructured the urban scene. Almost overnight, the train depot replaced the stage office as the nucleus of the city. After the first passenger station was built at Wynkoop and Twenty-second streets, saloon-keepers opened bars in the surrounding area to greet passengers. When Union Station was completed at Seventeenth and Wynkoop streets in 1881, Seventeenth Street emerged as the major commercial and tourist thor-oughfare, lined with hotels, banks, shops, and saloons (see map 2).

Saloonists sought locations as close to Union Station as possible.

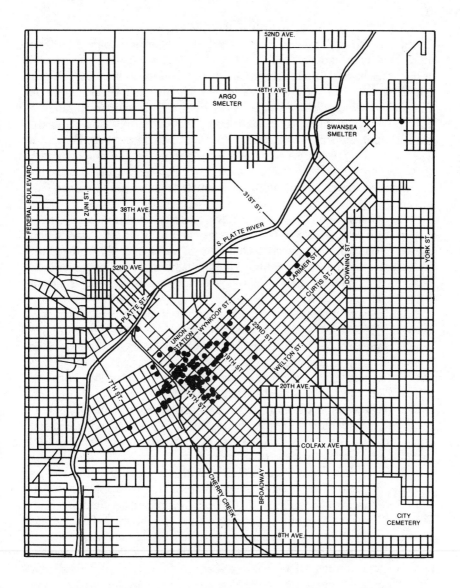

Map 2. Denver Saloons in 1880

George W. Schwenke leased a room inside the station and opened a saloon there. When the Denver, South Park and Pacific Railroad sought to expand its depot facilities, it found Schwenke's popular saloon in the way. After he refused to move out, the railroad started eviction proceedings and fenced off Schwenke's saloon. Schwenke, however, outfoxed the railroad by cutting a door-sized hole in the fence and tacking up the invitation, "Come and see me back of the fence." His customers continued to do just that. Perhaps it was the growing desperation of the railway people that led one night to a burst of gunfire directed at the saloon windows. Schwenke, asleep under his bar, escaped that blast but not an eviction order from the Colorado Supreme Court.[4]

Groggeries were also clustered in the trackside neighborhoods, where ore smelters; iron, steel, and brick factories; flour mills; beer breweries; and dozens of other industries were located. As railroads, industry, immigrants, and saloons became concentrated in these neighborhoods along the South Platte River bottoms, many middle- and upper-class Denverites began moving out of the city.

To facilitate urban flight, suburban land developers constructed, between 1871 and 1893, dozens of street railways, as streetcars were first called. Street railways enabled families to live outside the core city and yet retain quick, cheap, and easy access to its jobs, markets, and amusements. A nickel fare and a fifteen minute ride transported Denverites from the saloon-filled city to dry suburbs. Denver's first line, completed in 1871, carried passengers to the Curtis Park (later called Five Points) neighborhood, the first streetcar suburb and the place where moral geography first came into play. As Curtis Park became fashionable, other residential developments appeared in northeast Denver.

To serve these new neighborhoods, streetcar tracks branched off the Curtis Park line into the prairie, bringing homes and development in their wake. Lines went out East Fifteenth (Colfax), Seventeenth, Twenty-second, Twenty-fifth, Twenty-ninth, Thirty-first, Thirty-fourth, and Fortieth avenues, some reaching York Street, some pushing even farther east. Saloonkeepers and other entrepreneurs hoped to capitalize on the mushrooming new streetcar suburbs. "The growth of beer dives is keeping pace with the city's expansion," noted the *Rocky Mountain News* in the late 1880s, "and there has been much complaint of injury to new neighborhoods by the persistency with which those currupting dens are thrust in every available opening." After moving outside of the core city partly in order to escape such urban fixtures, suburbanites were distressed to find saloons moving into their new neighborhoods. Economic as well as moral considerations fueled the drive to exclude taverns, which homeowners condemned as "befouling and injurious to property values."[5]

In 1882 citizens began pressuring the Denver city council to ban saloons within five hundred feet of schools and churches. The city council managed to avoid doing this until 1889. Citizens also introduced a proposal in 1884 to limit saloons to one per block; but although neighborhood groups and antisaloonists brought the measure up repeatedly, it never passed the city council.[6]

Despite the promises of councilmen, liquor licenses continued to be awarded in new streetcar suburbs. In 1889, the city council sanctioned the proposed saloon of Timothy Connor, brother of a police lieutenant, in the Capitol Hill area, thus exciting "a turmoil in the neighborhood." Later that year, permission was "smuggled through the board of aldermen" to establish a bar in the most fashionable streetcar suburb of all, Capitol Hill. By 1890, the press reported that public sentiment was "working up to a white heat" against the movement of "beer dives into quiet residence neighborhoods."[7] In 1891, antisaloon suburbanites helped to elect Denver's first reform mayor, Platt Rogers, who promised to curb the power of the saloon.

If citizens in new streetcar additions to the city fretted about the "slimy saloon serpent," inhabitants of some suburban developments outside the city limits were even more outspoken. In their charters, ordinances, real estate prospectuses, and newspapers, the suburban towns boasted of being saloonless havens of morality, health, security, and prosperity (see map 3).

The town of Highlands sprang up around Denver's second streetcar line, which was constructed to North Denver in 1873. The "secrets of Highlands' success," according to the 1891 annual report for the town of seven thousand, were an elevated location above the smoke and smell of Denver, seven streetcar lines, and "NO SALOONS." By ordinance, Highlands defined liquor outlets as nuisances and established a prohibitively high annual license fee of five thousand dollars. A liquor license would not even be considered, according to another ordinance, without the approval of two-thirds of the landholders living within a half-mile radius.

To help prevent any seepage from the saloons and Zang Brewery of adjacent North Denver, Highlanders established a Woman's Christian Temperance Union reading room. The Committee of Fifty, a national research group dedicated to the scholarly investigation of "the liquor problem," claimed that "probably of all the social enterprises of the city of Denver, none have been so successful in drawing trade away from the saloon as the reading room."[8] The Committee of Fifty cited the case of a large streetcar barn built in Highlands which inspired the construction of two saloons across the street in Denver. The result, according to the Committee, was drunkenness among the streetcar employees, nourishment of neighborhood gangs, vandalism, and numerous disturbances. Then, in 1896, the WCTU established a reading room inside the "cheerless and cold" streetcar barn which attracted workers away from the saloons and forced one of them to close for lack of business.

Another saloonless town, Berkeley, flourished to the north of Highlands in the 1880s. If local authorities were lax about enforcing the town's

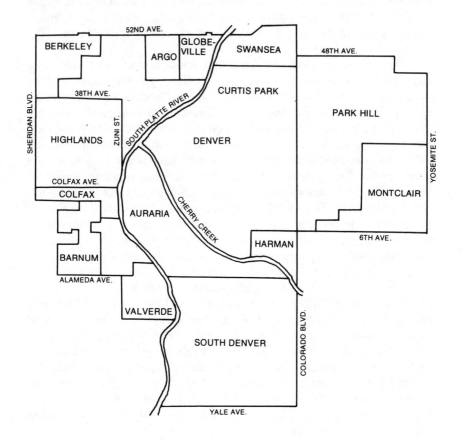

Map 3. Denver's Streetcar Suburbs

restrictive saloon license fee, two plume-hatted, black-skirted stalwarts of the Berkeley WCTU were vigilant. Hearing that a druggist was selling alcohol for nonmedicinal indulgence, this pair marched into his pharmacy. One of them complained of a cold, then bought a dime's worth of quinine and a quarter's worth of whiskey. Rather than mixing the quinine and whiskey, a legal remedy, the druggist poured the spirits into a separate bottle. The ladies triumphantly paraded their whiskey bottle before the magistrate, who fined the druggist two hundred dollars.[9]

In northeast Denver, Park Hill and Montclair were platted in the 1880s as dry suburbs for the upper crust. The prospectus for Downington, the most expensive section of Park Hill, contained "iron-clad restrictions" against schools and churches, as well as apartments, doubles [duplexes], hospitals, and stores. The prospectus did not bother to exclude saloons. It was written between the lines. After noting that Capitol Hill, then Denver's wealthiest neighborhood, had been defiled by commercial and multifamily dwellings, the Downington promoters assured lot buyers that they would never be " 'held-up' by the threat, either expressed or implied, to put up undesirable types of building on adjoining property." Amid Park Hill's parkways and croquet wickets, the children of Downington would "be free from the contaminating influence of down-town city streets."[10]

Playing on parental fears, the Downington prospectus continued: "Children with red blood in their veins resist the confining influence of cramped quarters in thickly settled districts. Are they to blame if they run out into the streets and get into bad company? Are they to blame if their delicate moral fibres are tarnished by evil associations? Is it not your duty to provide . . . for healthful and harmless recreation?"[11] Children in Downington and other Park Hill subdivisions supposedly had the best chance of developing high morals, outside the specter of the saloon.

Immediately south of Park Hill lay Montclair, platted by the Baron Walter von Richthofen shortly before his friend Baron von Winckler laid out Park Hill. Montclair, Richthofen declared in his 1885 prospectus for "The Beautiful Suburban Town of Denver," was to have "as pure a moral atmosphere and one as beneficial to society as the bracing air of Colorado. . . . Montclair should in effect be a club of families of congenial tastes, united for the purpose of excluding all that might destroy their peace or offend their better tastes."

Montclair deeds stipulated that intoxicants should never be manufactured, sold, or otherwise disposed of on the lots concerned. Temperance advocates in Montclair not only banned roadhouses, but also provided an alternative, a public water fountain. Denver, as Montclair officials noted during the dedication of the fountain near the junction of Richthofen Parkway and Oneida Street, contained hundreds of saloons but few public fountains.

To help keep their children away from Denver saloons, the town of

Montclair created its own school district in 1887. The *Montclair Mirror,* in an article probably aimed at Park Hill and Capitol Hill residents as well as locals, advised parents to send their children to Montclair High School rather than the East Denver High School "surrounded by saloons in the center of the city." Parents of East High School students shuddered at newspaper stories of beer halls luring students to drink. "A sweet young girl whose winning face and graceful form made her the idol," a typical article related, was "led into a wine room which, of course, meant seduction and ruin." After its incorporation as a separate town in 1888, Montclair established a twenty-five-hundred-dollar saloon license fee and other ordinances that kept the neighborhood saloonless. Any objectors had to do their barhopping at the Denver end of Montclair's two streetcar lines.[12]

South Denver was invaded by saloons early. When the 1882 National Mining and Industrial Exposition opened at Broadway and what is still known as Exposition Avenue, saloons sprang up like dandelions and lasted only a little longer. Of eleven taverns built near the exposition grounds, all but three had disappeared by the close of the show three years later. Yet some taverns survived and prospered with the expansion of the South Broadway streetcar, including Pop Wyman's roadhouse, Fiske's beer gardens, Broadway Park, and other resorts. Nearby Overland Park racetrack also attracted the sporting element, including Edward Chase, who set up a trackside beer and betting stand. Joseph Lowe and his wife, "Rowdy Kate," a couple infamous for the dance halls and bordellos they had run in other towns, opened the Cottage Grove in the 1880s. Nominally a beer garden, Cottage Grove was widely condemned as a disorderly house whose lewd, drunken regulars tarnished the image of South Denver.

The *Denver Eye,* the neighborhood's newspaper, took a dim view of these developments. Although South Denver was "destined to be filled with the homes of our best and most prominent citizens," the *Eye* observed that property was in danger of becoming "almost valueless because of these nuisances." At the urging of the *Eye* and some leading residents, South Denver began to reform itself.

The first step was setting up a local government. Although the town had been platted in 1874, it was not incorporated as a self-governing town until 1886. James Fleming, a Pennsylvania oilman who had become a Colorado mining man, contributed his mansion at 1520 South Grant Street as a town hall. He continued to live there after he became the town's first mayor, a post to which he was reelected three times. After the new government established thirty-five-hundred-dollar annual saloon license fee, the *Eye* boasted that South Denver's "roadhouses and saloons were all cleaned out, and it has remained free from these blots ever since."[13] On Denver's southwestern outskirts, the towns of Valverde and Barnum also used their charters and ordinances to curtail the number of saloons.

By 1890, Denver was virtually surrounded by saloonless suburbs. After growing with the city along its waterways, stage lines, and railways, the saloon was barred from following the path of the ultimate nineteenth-century city shaper, the streetcar. Between 1890 and 1915 taverns were largely confined to the core city and a few working-class and immigrant neighborhoods. Consequently, the tremendous growth in the number of saloons between 1880 and 1915, from some one hundred taverns to some five hundred, occurred primarily downtown. Although thousands of homes had been built in east Denver by 1900, only three saloons were tolerated there. Bars were also banned from the city's northwest quandrant bounded by West Colfax Avenue on the south and Zuni Street on the east. Except for a few taverns along Santa Fe Drive, Cherry Creek, and Broadway, the south side of town was also saloonless. While the city had mushroomed to 58.75 square miles by 1902, saloons remained concentrated in the 6-square-mile core city of the 1870s (see map 4).

After being banned in most of the Queen City's suburbs, taverns became concentrated along the downtown ends of the streetcar lines near the terminals, popular stops and transfer points. Between 1890 and 1915 several hundred saloons operated within the square-mile central business district bounded roughly by the Platte River on the west, Twenty-third Street on the north, Welton Street on the east, and Cherry Creek on the south (see map 5).

By 1890 Denver had more saloons per capita than Baltimore, Boston, Kansas City, Minneapolis, New Orleans, Philadelphia, St. Louis, or Washington. In 1890 the Mile-High City contained 478 saloons, or 4.48 bars per thousand people, according to the federal census bureau.[14] In the city's core, bars occupied nearly every corner. At Eighteenth and Curtis streets, the Killarney Cafe was surrounded by Pat O'Brien's L-shaped saloon, which had entrances on both streets. O'Brien's, the old-timers claimed, was so rough that the house would refund your money if you drank two beers and did not see a fight. Taverns were the most common business on many blocks of Market, Larimer, Fifteenth, Sixteenth, Seventeenth, Eighteenth, and Nineteenth streets.

Since barkeepers were often small businessmen—frequently blue-collar workers who had scraped together the minimal capital necessary for entrepreneurship—they sought the cheap-rent old buildings in the less fashionable downtown blocks. Bars often found homes in the oldest and most historic buildings, of which they were often the last occupants. When the Colorado National Bank moved out of its old quarters at Fifteenth and Market streets, Louis Schmidt rented the building for his Bank Saloon. The First National Bank's first home became the Meskew Brothers' Saloon. Austin M. Clark and E. H. Gruber's mint later housed a workingmen's tavern. The Wells Fargo office became a delicatessen, and the original First Baptist Church, was transformed into a German beer garden, Walhalla Hall.

Some turn-of-the-century saloons were located in the elegant old

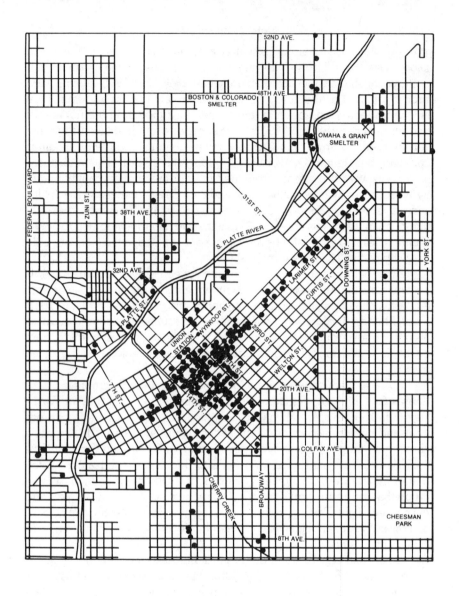

Map 4. Denver Saloons in 1900

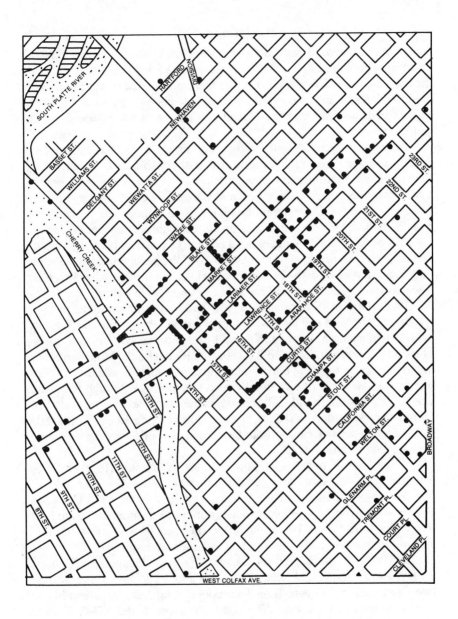

Map 5. Downtown Denver Saloons in 1900

downtown mansions of the wealthy who were moving out to the fashionable streetcar suburbs of Capitol Hill and Cheesman Park. Ed Chase converted the cupola-crowned William B. Daniels mansion at 1422 Curtis Street into the Inter-Ocean Club and refashioned the stately old school at Tremont Place and Broadway into the Navarre, a palace of wine, women, and gambling.

Although saloons were the most common urban institution, architecturally they were frequently among the least conspicuous. Freestanding saloons were commonly diminutive structures overpowered by neighboring hotels, business buildings, factories, and stores. The great majority of bars, however, were not freestanding buildings. Rather they were tucked into corners, buried in basements, stored up narrow flights of stairs, or hidden off the back alleys. Practically every hotel and major business block had a bar. Saloons could be found almost anywhere—in the basement of the Boston Building, in the lobby of the Brown Palace Hotel, in the alley behind the First National Bank, in a corner of the Tabor Grand Opera House.

Particularly after campaigns in the 1880s to enforce midnight and Sunday closing laws and the quickening of the prohibition crusade, saloons began maintaining a lower profile and inconspicuous side or back doors. Thus, on a spring Sunday in 1890, a reporter for the *Rocky Mountain News* found customers trooping into taverns through back and side doors. "Entrance was gained in one or two instances by passage through adjoining stores," the reporter found. "The crowds of bums and hangers-on seated on barrels outside served as guides to the inquisitive passerby."[15] To evade increasingly restrictive closing-hour laws, many saloons went underground decades before prohibition.

When Denver began aggressively annexing her suburbs after 1893, suburbanites made sure that most of the new areas would remain saloonless. Prohibitionist suburbs were legally sanctioned in an 1893 Colorado Supreme Court decision involving newly annexed Valverde. The court held that liquor traffic "may be prohibited in one part of a town or city and licensed in another part, as the public welfare may require."[16]

By 1902, Park Hill, South Denver, Harman, Highlands, Barnum, Colfax, Argo, Berkeley, Elyria, Globeville, Montclair, and Valverde had been annexed to Denver. Their incorporation significantly strengthened Denver's antisaloon minority. When Denverites went to the polls in 1914 to vote on the prohibition amendment, the six older city wards voted wet while six of the ten outlying wards voted dry to bolster the narrow statewide victory of prohibitionists. Suburbanites, after successfully banning the saloon at their end of the streetcar line, helped deliver all Coloradans into the dry promised land of their moral geography. After prohibition and to this day, the absence of bars is a hallmark of a "good neighborhood."

Denver's Demimonde

Denver's underworld was dominated by Edward Chase (left) almost from the time he arrived with the 1859 gold rush until his death in 1921. Chase, the son of a Saratoga Springs, New York, gambling house proprietor, opened his first Colorado sporting house in a tent.

Shortly afterward "Big Ed" built Colorado Territory's grandest gambling hall, the Progressive.

Colorado Historical Society

Sketch by T. R. Davis, Harper's Weekly, *Colorado Historical Society*

The Progressive mined the miners lucratively and gained notoriety after appearing on the front page of *Harper's Weekly* for February 7, 1866 (shown above).

In the 1870s, Chase replaced the Progressive Hall at Fifteenth and Blake streets with the 750-seat Palace Theatre. Nominally a theater, the Palace was better known for its vice and dice. It advertised the "Highest Limit in Denver" to attract heavy spenders. The Palace's crimson carpet, old timers said, hid gallons of blood from numerous fights and half a dozen murders. Theater performances leaned towards leg art; actresses served drinks between acts and entertained customers upstairs after the show. Among the actors listed on this playbill is the comedian Eddie Foy, later a star of the vaudeville stage.

Chase served on the city council in the 1860s but afterward retired to handle the vote in downtown wards from behind the scenes. Nearly every nineteenth-century election in Denver was clouded by charges that Chase had organized an army of voters out of riffraff, vagrants, prostitutes, barflies, and gamblers. This "saloonhall vote" frustrated reformers for decades.

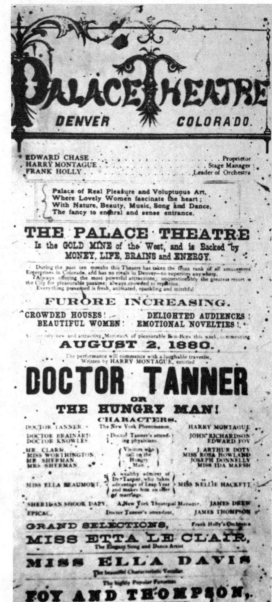

Districting of Arapahoe County by the Republican Leaders—"Planting

for Registration and Voting.

Political cartoonists portrayed Chase (center of cartoon at left) as the underworld boss, plotting election strategy with Bill Evans, head of the Denver Tramway Company, mine owner Bill Hamill, con man Soapy Smith, and other Republican party stalwarts.

From Rocky Mountain News, *Thomas J. Noel Collection*

Chase's last resort, the Navarre, is one of the few surviving nineteenth-century landmarks in downtown Denver. The Navarre, now on the National Register of Historic Places, opened in 1880 as a boarding school that restrained its female students from the "unprofitable and pernicious" practices of receiving male visitors or even corresponding with them.

A decade later, Chase converted the place to the Navarre and things were livelier in the old girls' school. Chase replaced the lace curtains with heavy red velvet drapes and the Navarre prospered. High-society sinners supposedly entered through a secret tunnel from the Brown Palace Hotel across Tremont Place. After Chase's death in 1921 the Navarre remained a café and night club that caught the eye of Denver artist Herndon Davis in 1940 (above). Now overshadowed by skyscrapers in the heart of downtown Denver, the Navarre is a reminder of Denver's shady past and of the gambler who helped shape the city's political and social life.

Denver had seven males per female in 1860. The ratio had changed by 1900, when women slightly outnumbered men. Yet prostitutes continued to be fixtures in many saloons. Ed Chase used women to attract customers, but he had no monopoly on the use of coy waitresses, dance girls, and prostitutes. California Hall, catercorner from City Hall on Larimer Street, was a notorious dive that thrived until demolition in 1902, despite frequent closings for "allowing

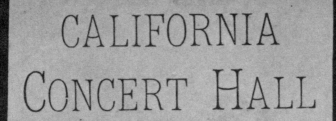

CALIFORNIA CONCERT HALL

DENVER, COLO.

——

This House engages only the very best and

Highest Salaried People in the Profession

and claims to give the

Brightest, Cleanest and Most Refined

SPECIALTY SHOW IN AMERICA.

——

Admission, To all Parts of the House, **25c.**

immoral, vulgar and blasphemous females to assemble in said place for the purpose of attracting customers."

The two-sided California Hall card is one of the few surviving invitations. Once dozens of lower downtown saloons distributed such calling cards, but they were not the kind of souvenirs that a man kept around the house or buried in grandfather's trunk.

COME AND SEE ME AT

CALIFORNIA CONCERT HALL

Jim Wright Collection

Chapter 8
SYNDICATES
AND THE SEAMY SIDE

Although exaggerated, suburban fears of saloon abuses were not unfounded. At the turn of the century, liquor was becoming a big business that many associated with alcoholism, gambling, prostitution, crime, poverty, and poor health. Consequently, prohibitionists could effectively make the saloon a scapegoat for many economic and social abuses.

In an age when Presidents Theodore Roosevelt, William Howard Taft, and Woodrow Wilson all preached or practiced "trust-busting," the liquor industry soon came under attack as one of the "malefactors of great wealth." Liquor men, like many other American businessmen, attempted to eliminate or combine with competitors in a monopolistic trend toward regional, national, and international corporate consolidation. When large and often remote corporations gained ownership or financial control of neighborhood bars and "mom and pop" saloons, prohibitionists found their work easier. They could attack out-of-town, out-of-state, and foreign rum sellers more comfortably than they could campaign against locally owned businesses.

British efforts to monopolize American brewing in the 1880s led to much tighter competition. Pabst and Schlitz of Milwaukee, Lemp and Anheuser-Busch of St. Louis, and Lemp of Chicago began aggressive nationwide sales and saloon-buying campaigns. By 1900, half of the Queen City's taverns were owned by Denver-, Chicago-, St. Louis-, Milwaukee- or London-based breweries.[1]

In trying to control all stages of the industry, from production to retail sales, breweries bought saloons or arranged mortgages, loans, and other financial commitments that would tie saloonkeepers to their products. Sometimes, breweries resorted to strong-arm tactics, sending thugs into saloons to intimidate proprietors, as a March 28, 1892, story in the *Rocky Mountain News* illustrated.

> "Gimme some beer."
>
> The bartender grasps a glass, fills it with the foaming fluid and slides it along the polished counter with that peculiar flip which causes it to swing around, handle outward.
>
> The customer swallows down half the contents of the glass hastily, as does a man used to malt liquors, then a pained expression spreads over his face, he expels whatever portion of beer remains in his mouth and places the glass back on the bar with outward indication of inward disgust.
>
> "What kind of slop is that?"
>
> "That's Western Brewery beer."
>
> "Ain't you got Zang's?"
>
> "No."
>
> "That settles it; I ain't huntin' no dishwater to drink." Out stomps the customer, while the proprietor thoughtfully mops the bar with his apron.

As this often repeated episode suggests, rivalry became fierce in Denver. The beer battle became particularly bitter after an English syndicate purchased the locally owned Zang Brewery and the Denver Brewing Company in 1889 for $2.5 million. Although Philip Zang's first love was the brewery he founded, his son Adolph became more interested in other family ventures, including the German National Bank and the Oxford Hotel. Adolph continued only as the figurehead of the brewery, which had become a subsidiary of Denver United Breweries, Ltd. New ownership had been arranged with the help of James Duff, a shrewd Scot who brought British investors into many facets of Denver's economy during the 1880s. After moving into Denver, the London-based firm began testing Adolph Zang's proposition that in the beer business "any new competitor can be crushed out for $10,000."[2]

A few other breweries survived the tightening competition. Frederick Neef bought out the old Western Brewery in 1891 and renamed it Neef Brothers Brewery. His business survived until prohibition, when it collapsed after failing to profitably manufacture near beer. Adolph Coors—whose name still remains carved over the doors of some Denver bars—and a partner founded their brewery in a Golden tannery in 1873. The following year Coors was appraised by the R. G. Dun and Company as "a young man of good character & habits . . . a practical brewer [with] but little means." After one false start, Coors had acquired the financial support of Jacob Schuler. Despite tough competition from the Denver brewers, Coors's operation survived by specializing in bottled lager, which could readily be shipped to mountain mining towns and prairie farming hamlets.[3]

In 1901, the newly consolidated Tivoli-Union Brewery joined the beer battle. John Good, one-time proprietor of the Rocky Mountain Brewery, put together the Tivoli-Union. Good had sold his old Rocky Mountain Brewery to its manager, Philip Zang, but remained active in several brewing companies. Good's Tivoli-Union was the corporate descendant of numerous Denver breweries, including Max Melsheimer's Milwaukee Brewery, City Brewery, Boerchert's Brewery, and the Tivoli. For his plant, Good chose the large and distinctive building at Tenth and Larimer streets. Soon the Tivoli-Union was second only to Zang's in production and sales. The Tivoli-Union, which stayed in business until 1969, outlasted all competitors except Adolph Coors. Coors celebrated its centennial in 1973, claiming to be the largest single-plant brewery in the United States.

Two technological advances in the brewers' art enabled out-of-state firms to compete in Colorado. Pasteurization of lager beer made possible long-range shipment with minimum spoilage, as did the crown cap, which replaced corks and ceramic seals with a gas-tight, cork-lined metal cap. Along with improved railroad transportation, these improvements helped to bring Budweiser, Pabst, Schlitz, and Blatz to the Mile High City by 1900.

Larger, more efficient breweries also profited from the nationwide depression of 1893, which wiped out many competitors and reduced the number of Colorado breweries from twenty-three in 1893 to sixteen in 1895. Of Denver's numerous preprohibition breweries, only six lasted until 1915. To survive, brewers sought to control the saloons, where beer easily outstripped hard liquor in popularity by 1900, with wines taking a distant third place.

Beer barons not only granted credit and chattel mortgages to saloonkeepers but also began to buy bar licenses, land, buildings, and entire businesses. High license fees, passed by prohibitionists to drive bars out of business, often drove bars into the hands of wealthy brewery magnates. By 1900 Blatz and Schlitz, as well as Zang, Neef, and Tivoli-Union, held local saloon licenses. Adolph Coors's brewery in nearby Golden also began collecting saloons.

Beer merchants put the squeeze on independent saloonkeepers, as Benjamin Hurwitz, a leading Larimer Street purveyor, discovered. To satisfy his brewery debts, Hurwitz had to sell one of his bars to Tivoli-Union for eleven hundred dollars. Two years later, in 1906, the still-indebted Jewish proprietor mortgaged all of his bar fixtures, including his prized deer heads, brass footrail, nine brass cuspidors, and mahogany backbar, to cover an overdue thirty-five-hundred-dollar debt to Tivoli-Union. Saloonkeepers such as Hurwitz complained that they spent their lives struggling for independence, only to be driven more deeply into brewery debt by climbing license fees, wholesale liquor costs, building overhead and tight competition.[4]

A 1907 legal agreement between Hurwitz and the brewery provided him with a loan of almost $3,000 at 10 percent a year, due in eighteen months. In addition, Hurwitz had to buy only Tivoli-Union beer at $6.50 a barrel. Pushing Hurwitz to sell as much of their brew as possible, his creditors promised him a credit of 50¢ for each barrel he bought. Even after he paid off the loan, Tivoli agreed to return his license and lease only if Hurwitz continued to market their beer exclusively. Whether he liked it or not, Hurwitz was a Tivoli man.

The problems of independent saloonists inspired Benjamin Hurwitz to play a leading role in the establishment of the Denver Saloonkeepers' Union No. 1 in 1907. This union sought to defend its members against both brewery exploitation and rising public criticism. Hoping to enhance the profession's image, Hurwitz and the union attempted to divorce the saloon from politics, since that marriage had fostered much antisaloon sentiment. Hurwitz drew up and the saloonkeepers' union sponsored a ballot petition for a change in the city charter, entitled "An Amendment Taking the Saloon Out of Politics." Hurwitz claimed that bar owners were forced into political activism by the Fire and Police Board, which had arbitrary authority to revoke bar licenses and to refuse to relicense any saloon. City hall used this authority to force saloonkeepers to contribute cash and votes. The "saloon-out-of-politics" amendment passed in the 1912 spring election. It required jury trials to revoke a license and provided for automatic relicensing of bars unless unlawful conduct could be proven.

Passing the charter amendment was one of the few successes of Saloonkeepers' Union No. 1. Confronted by greedy brewers, corrupt politicians, and an increasingly critical public, the saloonists faced a bleak future. Even if licensed proprietors wanted to improve the profession's image, they could not get the city to close hundreds of unlicensed bars that played politics to stay open. "Can we afford to enter a competition for our existence, handicapped with the weight of odium caused by over 500 bootleggers?" the union's executive board wrote to the city safety commissioner in 1914, begging him to crack down on the illegal outlets.[5] Thanks to both self-reform and imposed reform, Denver saloons were probably politically cleaner on the eve of prohibiton than they ever had been. Yet liquor men failed to make this point effectively in their struggle against the dry crusade.

Hurwitz appreciated the irony: small-time saloons were being condemned by vote-hungry politicians who clandestinely continued to solicit dram-shop payoffs and were being financially crushed by brewery barons who espoused the virtues of free enterprise. Benjamin Hurwitz, like hundreds of other turn-of-the-century reformers disillusioned with capitalism, turned to socialism. He and his brother became leaders of Colorado's Socialist Labor party, which held many of its meetings in Hurwitz's saloon.

Denver saloonkeepers proved no match for the brewery barons. In 1913, Hurwitz received a letter from his close friend George Becherer, proprietor of the Mining Exchange Bar at Fifteenth and Arapahoe streets. After twelve years in the Denver saloon business, Becherer notified friends and creditors, "I have been forced to surrender my place of business to the Zang Brewing Company, the holder of the mortgage against the fixtures in my property." Becherer begged his creditors to leave him his remaining liquor stock "and the trifle that could be realized therefrom. . . . If this can be granted me, I will not be, as I now am, utterly penniless." Federal district court bankruptcy dockets disclose that many other saloonkeepers were also struggling to keep even their hats, underwear, and handkerchiefs out of creditors' hands.[6]

Once the breweries drove men like Becherer out of business, they put their newly acquired outlets into the hands of amenable agents. These company saloons, operating under pressure to sell as much liquor as possible gave all saloons a bad name. "This class of place, set up and controlled by the breweries," complained the *Rocky Mountain News*, "are as a rule the worst." State investigators reached the same conclusion, finding that the company liquor sellers were commonly men "of the worst character" who could never qualify for a license of their own. The state investigators condemned Denver's "pernicious practice" of allowing one company to take out numerous licenses.[7] Even after prohibition, the memory of abusive monopolies and brewery syndicates led to stipulations—still in effect in Colorado and elsewhere—against the ownership of more than one saloon or the ownership of saloons by breweries.

Groggeries standing side by side in lower downtown Denver competed desperately, often by offering seductive women (or pictures thereof), gambling, and other vices. Particularly in the brewery-owned bars, the saloonkeeper was no longer an independent neighborhood merchant likely to take pride in his reputation and show concern for his customers. Rather, he was the easily replaceable agent. His employers did not care how well he polished the mahogany so long as he shoved drinks across it. Barkeepers sold liquor to minors, women, and inebriates, confident that their bosses in the liquor industry could protect them at city hall.

Depravity had always existed in Denver saloons, but mounting public outrage led Governor James H. Peabody to order an investigation of abuses in 1903. On their late-night probes, state agents reported excesses and illegalities. Inside the Ghost Block building at Fifteenth and Glenarm streets, they found inebriated, half-dressed women and men cavorting. If orgies were staged inside bars uptown, they spilled into the streets of lower downtown Denver. Investigators had to fight their way through crapulous crowds to enter downtown dens of iniquity. The saloon snoopers elbowed into Goodman's at Eighteenth and Larimer streets and found it a filthy place inhabited by both adults and minors described as "bums, dirty and disreputable in appearance and with bloated faces." Semiconscious, lumpish patrons sat on planks and barrels swilling quart schooners. In the basement of the White House Saloon, the investigators found tipsy men, women, and children engaged in "obscene behavior." The "most shocking sight" of the night, at Klipfel's bar at Twentieth and Market streets, was "a drunken white woman being drug into the wine rooms by niggers, all using the most vile and obscene language." In bar after bar, Bacchus reigned.[8]

While drunkenness had been tolerated in the nineteenth century, early-twentieth-century idealists publicized it as a matter of civic concern. Reformers argued that drunkenness and associated vices should not be tolerated but eliminated. Alcoholism, the public was told, was a curable disease. One indication of this change in public opinion was the appearance of drink-cure institutes in Denver and other cities. Some, such as the Keeley Institute, promised "an absolute and permanent cure for alcoholics." Colorado became one of the first states to provide medical care for alcoholics and soon afterward the director of the state insane asylum complained that Denver was dumping too many "drunkards or cases of alcoholism" into his hands. Denver police reported that drunkenness accounted for a fifth of the city's arrests and listed it as a leading cause of death.[9]

Employers also complained that alcoholism was a serious problem. Denver's worst accident of the nineteenth century, a boiler explosion in the Gumry Hotel that killed twenty-two guests, happened while the on-duty boiler engineer sat in a nearby tavern. The Colorado Fuel and Iron Company had to shut down its plants for days at a time after paydays because of employee drinking sprees. Heavy drinking among railroad workers led the American Railway Association to pass a rule forbidding employees to drink on the job or frequent places where intoxicants were sold.

If the monotony of industrial jobs drove men to drink, the machinery they operated made it hazardous to do so. A national committee investigating the liquor problem concluded that

> the necessity of having a clear head during the hours of labor becomes imperative, and the very conditions of modern life necessitate sobriety on the part of workers . . . as more things are done by machinery, as trolley-cars supplement horse-cars, as implements of greater precision and refinement take the place of cruder ones, as the speed at which machinery is run is increased, as the intensity with which people work becomes greater.

Alcohol, other investigators reported, was responsible for many of the thirty-five thousand deaths and two hundred thousand accidents that annually plagued American industry.[10]

Not only employers but also some union leaders found saloongoing a curse of the working classes. "If we workers were all sober," one labor leader postulated, "we would be on top of the social heap within five years." The *Horseshoer's Magazine,* published in Denver for the national organization, declared that in an up-to-date 1907 horseshoeing shop "there should be no going out to drink in working hours by boss or journeyman and all drinking should be done at noon hour and after work unless a visiting horseshoer should call and take all hands out for a drink."[11]

As the horseshoers' anticipation of free drinks from visitors suggests, many workingmen cherished the saloon, even if drinking increased accidents among their ranks. "The saloon exists in our town," one workingman wrote to the *Miners' Magazine* of the Western Federation of Miners in June 1912, "because it supplies a want—a need. It offers a common meeting place. It dispenses good cheer. It ministers to the craving for fellowship. To the exhausted, worn out body, to the strained nerves—the relaxation brings rest."

William "Big Bill" Haywood, editor of the Denver-based *Miners' Magazine,* scoffed at prohibition. He called it a capitalistic scheme to pile up "more profits through greater physical efficiency and endurance on the part of the slaves." Haywood's defiance suggests an unarticulated but probably deep-seated explanation of excessive drinking among wageworkers: drinking was a form of social protest against miserable working conditions.

For whatever reason, many workers did enjoy their cups and drunkenness became an undeniable problem. Rather than encourage moderation, most barmen and barmaids continually extended the invitation, "Another round?" The man who dropped in just to wet his whistle rarely left after one drink if he found treating friends. Barroom chivalry obligated him to accept drinks purchased for him and to stay long enough to buy at least one round. John C. Osgood, the idealistic head of the Colorado Fuel and Iron Company, found that saloons were "necessary" for the working class, but tried to upgrade them by adding reading rooms and discouraging the practice of treating.[12]

Anyone doubting that tippling houses harbored heavy drinkers did not have far to look for proof. In almost any Denver saloon, the human tragedies portrayed in melodramas such as *The Drunkard* and *Ten Nights in a Barroom* were acted out nightly. Even when it would have been in their best interest, many barkeeps refused to stop the show. Their shortsighted obsession with selling another nickel beer helped in the long run to kill the multimillion-dollar liquor industry.

The tavern was also censured as a haven for labor agitators, as a working men's club that harbored union activity. Eugene Debs, founder and president of the American Railway Union and America's star socialist, chose a saloon as his public platform in Denver. The lanky, amiable Debs was quickly ushered through the Larimer Street saloon of fellow socialist Benjamin Hurwitz to the upstairs hall and not allowed to linger at the bar and forget about his speech.

Organizers like Debs and "Big Bill" Haywood relied on bars as recruitment centers, meeting halls, and strike headquarters. The 1903 Globeville smelter strike spilled into the street from a popular workingmen's tavern.

Although it was blamed on Haywood and other high-spirited barroom organizers, the strike was a response to long work days, poor pay, and dangerous working conditions. When Haywood and the Western Federation of Miners organized the Denver Mill and Smelter Workers, men worked ten- or twelve-hour days for wages ranging from $1.75 a day for common laborers to $2.75 for furnace men. On July 3, 1903, workers walked out of the Globe and Grant smelters, leaving furnaces full of hot ore to freeze and destroy thousands of dollars' worth of equipment. Haywood declared that only a three-dollar-a-day minimum wage and an eight-hour day would bring employees back to work.[13]

Smelter owners responded by calling in antiunion law enforcement officials. After police arrested six strikers, a crowd gathered at John Predovich's place. Predovich, the police charged, was more adamant than any of the union men in urging the crowd to rescue their jailed companions. When a patrol wagon arrived, strikers reportedly shouted, "Get your guns and kill them." Police arrested Predovich and three others. In the Denver jail, the Croatian-born saloonkeeper confessed to advising his customers to free the strike prisoners because they were friends of his. Another Globeville mixologist, Max Malich, posted bond for Predovich and the other prisoners.[14]

The protest at Predovich's was suppressed and all other taverns in Globeville were closed. The strike, however, was not so quickly snuffed. It simmered throughout the long, hot summer. Not until November was it extinguished by a court injunction against picketing and by the efforts of Denver's Citizens' Protective Alliance, a vigilante-style coalition of capitalists that helped prosecute strikers and protect strikebreakers.

During the following decade of industrial warfare in Colorado, saloons were condemned as havens of labor unrest. When strikes broke out, authorities regularly closed all taverns in the area, hoping to eliminate support for the workers. By linking the saloon to the labor movement, both antisaloonists and antiunionists advanced their causes.

Saloons also attracted public condemnation because of their close ties with prostitution. The *Rocky Mountain News* for July 23, 1889, expressed the widely held view that beer halls were "the most fruitful source for breeding and feeding prostitution." Despite ordinances passed as early as 1870 against the use of women to attract male customers, saloonkeepers consistently relied on waitresses, dancers, bar girls, and prostitutes to bring in male patrons. During the 1880s, public controversy focused on the so-called wine rooms. Proprietors contended that the rooms provided couples with a separate outside entrance into secluded backrooms away from the smoke, noise, and roughhousing of the front-room bar. Operating under this guise of respectability, wine rooms opened in sections of Denver that would never have tolerated brothels. Bar owners lined their back halls with wine rooms furnished with horsehair sofas, tables, and chairs. Reformers grew suspicious as they watched bartenders slip drinks to couples behind closed doors.

Responding to widespread indignation, the Colorado General Assembly passed a law in 1891:

> That no saloon, tippling house, or dram shop shall have or keep in connection with or as a part of such saloon, tippling house, or dram shop any wine room or other place either with or without door or doors, curtain or curtains or screen of any kind into which any female persons shall be permitted to enter from the outside or from such saloon, tippling house or dram shop and there be supplied with any kind of liquor whatsoever.[15]

Some feminists joined saloonkeepers in protesting this law, and they convinced Arapahoe County Judge Robert W. Steele that it infringed on women's rights. In 1897, Judge Steele ruled that women should be permitted wine with meals.

The resultant revival of wine rooms led to some unladylike behavior, as a state investigator testified four years later. After following a woman and small child through the ladies' entrance to the Log Cabin at Fifteenth and Larimer streets, the detective found male customers watching "a woman playing with a dog in an obscene manner." Another male huddle surrounded "a little girl about twelve years old" being held up by her heels and spanked. Reports of such activities and occasional complaints about pornography and venereal disease lent weight to denunciations of the saloon as a seducing ground.[16]

If some saloons doubled as brothels, Denver's numerous brothels also doubled as saloons. Some bawds, such as Mattie Silks, had liquor licenses, but unlicensed whorehouses also served alcohol, charging exorbitant prices for nose paint, tonsil varnish, and tongue oil, as wags called the ardent. A split of champagne supposedly cost as much as one hundred dollars. A pocket directory that appeared in 1892, *A Reliable Directory of the Pleasure Resorts of Denver,* contained parlor-house advertisements boasting of "boarders" who cordially welcomed strangers. Among the amenities usually listed were choice wines and liquors.

Unlike the more discreet wine rooms, the garish Market Street district conducted business openly. Residents and visitors alike took frequent strolls down that street (originally called McGaa Street, then Holladay Street from 1866 to 1889, when the name was changed to Market at the request of the indignant Holladay family). On weekend nights hundreds of men and boys jammed what Denverites called "the line." Between Nineteenth and Twenty-third streets, the red-light row glowed with illuminated signs bearing invitations such as "Men Taken In and Done For."[17] From doorways, windows, and couches in brightly lighted parlors, women purred their invitations. Anyone rude enough to walk by these damsels without at least passing the time of day might have his hat snatched. Then even the most reluctant gentlemen would have to go inside to redeem his chapeau. As early as 1880 and as late as 1912, hundreds of soiled doves conducted business on Market Street. After reform Mayor Henry J. Arnold took office in 1912, he permanently closed the Market Street district.

Not all saloonhall sex was commercial. Various Denver dance halls catered to young couples and singles with band music and the promise of companionship. Once girls took their first sip of liquor, prohibitionists declared, they were ruined. Judge Ben Lindsey, in his seamy side strolls, found "indescribable" activities in dance halls. Three girls enticed into one saloon were found the next day naked and groaning in a cellar. When Judge Lindsey investigated such cases he found that the dive keepers had been promised immunity from police interference because of their contributions to Mayor Speer's campaign chest.[18]

Utlimately dance halls were subjected to special licensing and supervision by police matrons and Denver's first woman police detective, social worker Josephine Roche, who was named inspector of public amusements. Miss Roche reprimanded overly amorous young people and became noted for her ability to pacify honky-tonk brawlers. She tried to enforce a new law that required dance hall owners to record the names and addresses of all patrons under twenty-one and see that they were escorted home by parents or guardians before 10:00 P.M.

Miss Roche had less luck policing wine rooms. She filed a complaint against a wine room owned in part by the safety inspector. Shortly thereafter, she was asked to resign from the police force and Denver's nationally acclaimed program to preserve civic virtue and virgins was abandoned. Miss Roche subsequently ran for governor of Colorado and became President Franklin Delano Roosevelt's assistant secretary of the treasury and president of the Rocky Mountain Fuel Company. Wine rooms and dance halls thrived in her absence.[19]

If a man encountered a woman in a preprohibition saloon, he might well suspect her virtue. For saloon going remained not only legally but socially taboo for women until speakeasies became fashionable among middle- and upper-class women during the 1920s. Respectable Denver women, in common with their fallen sisters on Market Street, often chose narcotics instead of alcohol. "Opium eating," a Colorado physician contended in 1880, "is the growing and fashionable vice among the rich—especially the fashionable women, who, in the giddy round of evanescent pleasure, must have stimulant. Whiskey and champagne are painful in their after effects rather than pleasant. Beer is vulgar and it fattens and no fashionable lady wants to be fat." In 1903 the *Denver Medical Times* reported that women outnumbered men by more than ten to one as opium users.[20]

Ladies reluctant to drink in public sometimes sent children to fetch beer for them in coffee cans and milk pails. The youngsters would slip in a side door and get in line to fill the can. On the way back, children came up with a game to play—trying to swing the pails in a full circle without spilling the suds.

If old photographs and police records are any indication, children frequented bars more often before prohibition than after. Sometimes youngsters rushed beer buckets to homebound drinkers or supplied their seniors in the shop or on the work crew. Other minors imitated adults by simply loitering in bars, which were mysterious and fascinating places for many children. Something always seemed to be happening—gambling, singing, fighting, dancing, or at least a game of pool or tenpins. A favorite game was to slip into the Silver Dollar and try to pry loose the coins imbedded in the floor. Denver's juvenile gangs, like the feared River Front bunch, hung around bars plotting mischief and crimes, rolling drunks, and fleecing greenhorns. Minors frequented taverns regularly, knowing that only a few token arrests occurred each year; it was hard to prove that children in a bar had been drinking. Later laws penalized saloonkeepers for even admitting minors.[21]

Occasionally juveniles became the victims of what the newspapers called "unspeakable" and "unnatural" crimes involving what may have been early homosexual bars. One fifteen-year-old lad was befriended by a patron of the Moses Home, a Fifteenth Street saloon. After promising to find a job for the boy, the man took him "down into the brush near the railroad track back of Mullen's flouring mill. . . . the man picked up a heavy stick and compelled the boy to take off his clothing. The man, or more properly, the fiend, then committed on the boy that which the state statutes describe as the crime against nature, and other revolting outrages of a similar character."[22] Half a dozen plainclothesmen scoured the city for the "fiend" before finding that he had returned to the Moses Home.

Newspaper-reading Denverites regularly encountered lurid tales of saloons where girls were deflowered or boys were subjected to "unspeakable" crimes, where men were murdered and women led to a fate worse than death. Such publicized depravity in the city's worst saloons made it difficult for more respectable drinking houses to defend their existence. Of his criminal cases, one judge declared that "95 per cent of them were due to liquor purchased in saloons." The *Rocky Mountain News* attributed 80 percent of the Queen City's violent crime to liquor. Revenue from bars, the newspaper added, was less than the money spent on policing, trying, and jailing criminals "manufactured by the saloon." Critics trying to link bars and crime could also point out that the numerous watering spots surrounding the city jail were often headquarters for bail bondsmen as well as the criminals they assisted. Bondsmen found taverns convenient as they were commonly open late at night and had safes.[23]

Accusations of saloon-inspired criminality probably were exaggerated, but some bars were the scene of fights, murders, con games, and fencing operations. The "King of the Con Men," Jefferson Randolph "Soapy" Smith, was a southern dandy who wore three-piece black suits, diamond stick pins, and a gold pocket watch and chain. After setting up a stand at Seventeenth and Larimer streets, Smith began haranguing the masses about their lack of cleanliness and promoting "the finest soap in the world, perfected in my own laboratory, and manufactured in my own factory." Lukewarm response greeted Soapy's exhortations that "cleanliness is next to godliness," until he began inserting dollar bills into some of the soap-cake wrappers. Inevitably the bills went to Soapy's confederates, but the crowds never tired of hearing this slippery huckster lie through his luxurious beard. With proceeds from his dollar-a-cake soap business, Soapy opened the Tivoli Saloon and gambling hall at Seventeenth and Market streets. "Caveat Emptor," read Soapy's doorway sign. He was confident that few of his customers knew Latin.[24]

In some of the worst doggeries, customers felt naked without firearms. Several Larimer Street resorts seemed to relish their criminal reputations: Walker's was dubbed the "Bucket of Blood" and Murphy's was christened the "Slaughterhouse." Three homicides took place inside Ed Chase's Palace in one year. Several taverns specialized in swindling customers, who woke up in toilet rooms or back alleys to find their money gone. Certain tavernkeepers, as their victims testified in court, drugged or encouraged patrons to inebriation and then robbed them. Out-of-town visitors were fleeced so often that Denver gained an unsavory reputation for thieves and bunco artists. "When the average country merchant does summon sufficient courage to visit this city," one *Rocky Mountain News* editorial complained, "he sews his wad of money in his vest lining, takes an affectionate last farewell of his family and friends, leaves directions as to the color he would prefer to have his tombstone painted every summer, and boards the train, filled with the certainty that who enters Denver leaves hope behind."[25]

Those robbed in saloons might later have a chance to buy back their possessions at a fraction of the original cost in the same bar. Thieves often used saloons for selling stolen horses, bicycles, watches, weapons, jewelry, and other merchandise. A ring of horsethieves operated out of one of Ed Chase's saloons until the case was cracked by David Cook, Colorado's most famous private detective. After spending several days playing Spanish Monte with suspects "Smiley" and "Goggle-eyed Ed," Cook deduced that they bought army horses from soldiers who delivered them to a nearby saloon late at night. Another long-time Denver detective, Sam Howe, also found stolen goods sold and stored in drinking houses.[26]

Drunkenness reigned among tavern indiscretions. The lack of stools at nineteenth-century bars, which could make it dramatically evident when tipplers could no longer stand up, was one of the few tactics that could be used to discourage excessive drinking. They might then be dragged outdoors or to an unoccupied nook in the room. Long after the frontier period passed, heavy drinking remained an expression of hospitality and of manliness. The obsession with virility, potency, body building, and sports that characterized turn-of-the-century America permeated saloons. At the bar, men were often expected to assert their manhood by exhibiting their drinking capacity.

Foreign-born men may have felt a greater need to retire to haunts such as saloons and assert masculine values because women in America had more rights, more nondomestic jobs, more money, and more control over men than in many countries. Masculine language, dress, and behavior were expected inside the swinging doors. Saloons also might be cluttered with pictures of military and athletic heroes who were considered models for emulation.

Industrial workers patronized saloons heavily, often on a daily basis, seeking a change from the hardships of work and poverty-plagued households. As a depressant, alcohol reduced inhibitions and social distance, enabling workingmen to share experiences with coworkers, barroom acquaintances, or at least with the bartender. The saloon served as a counseling center, as group therapy, and as a confessional.

Ritualistic, if informal, meetings began with invitations to join a work group for a round of libations. Both veterans and newcomers were expected to join in "bottoms up" toasts. Not to drink with one's colleagues was considered unfriendly and inimicable to work relationships, promotions, and job security.[27]

For drinking sprees, whoring, crime, business and labor meetings, and other activities, Denverites, other Coloradans, and visitors resorted to the Queen City's numerous bars. Denver became a binge town, a city where bars catered to visitors from surrounding mines, ranches, railroads, military bases, and farms. As the city grew to well over two hundred thousand by 1910, it became not only the commercial but also the amusement hub of the Rocky Mountain region, with the reputation of being one of the wildest cities in the West.

Many drinkers and drink merchants relished Denver's reputation, but others suspected that either reform or prohibition lay ahead. A few saloon owners appreciated the intensity of the dry crusade and tried to change with the times. Some, well aware that the bar business had a seamy side, tried to improve the image of the saloon and its clientele. Changing the conduct of their patrons proved difficult. The lack of restraints and the broad tolerance of behavior that would be unacceptable elsewhere were precisely what attracted many patrons. The saloon, its keepers, and its patrons never changed enough to accommodate disapproving public attitudes.

Etiquette books never stooped to prescribing beer-parlor behavior. Yet some proprietors tried gentle suggestions, posting signs such as "If you spit on the floor at home, spit on the floor here. We want you to feel at home."

91

Spitting, however, remained part of saloon vocabulary—a forceful expression of disdain or an invitation to combat. Usually there were cuspidors and sawdust on the floor anyway. Some tobacco chewers continued to mouth their cuds while they imbibed, claiming that the juice added flavor to their alcohol. As they drank, chewers grew bolder about their ability to hit the cuspidor at long range. Consequently the brown puddle around the spittoons grew larger as the night wore on, staining even the most elegant rugs, tile, and marble. For protection, some bar owners placed sand around the stoves at which stove sharks fired to hear the sizzle. Men behind the mahogany were never noted for their optimism about the perfectability of human nature.

Many tavernkeepers posted signs that they hoped would get the message across, such as "Please don't shoot the Piano Player—He's doing the best he can." Some tavernkeepers tried to enforce ordinances against discharging firearms within the city limits or "any drunkenness, quarreling, fighting, unlawful games, or disorderly conduct whatsoever." Barkeepers usually attempted to shove brawlers outside before they could smash up the furniture and each other. This could be dangerous: bar men were often mauled and even murdered. One barkeeper's solution was to charge troublemakers a dollar extra for each drink.[28]

It was easier, saloonkeepers found, to improve the premises than to improve the manners of patrons. Some of them tried to upgrade the patronage by sprucing up their buildings and raising their prices. The best resorts remodeled frequently and decorated lavishly to court the respectable. Proprietors added awnings and curtains, installed chandeliers and candelabra, and replaced paintings of nudes and mounted animal heads with genteel landscapes and potted plants. Of course not all the paintings of nudes disappeared, and some bar gazers found refinements. One nude reportedly had rubber hoses hooked up to the back of her canvas belly and bosom. By pumping the air bulb at the end of the hoses, the bartender delighted regulars and befuddled visitors.

The Windsor Hotel bar had a floor of black walnut and white ash and a bar of Colorado pine and California redwood. A huge 90-by-120-foot mirror reflected the three thousand silver dollars placed in the floor, the bentwood chairs, the elegant billiard parlor, and distinguished visitors. Among the latter was Buffalo Bill Cody, who, after being limited to ten drinks a day, reportedly talked the bartender into putting his shots into a beer stein.

Frank Edbrooke, the city's leading architect, included a pub in the grandiose opera house he designed for silver magnate Horace Tabor. "A scene of splendor and magnificence unequalled in the United States," raved the *Denver Republican* on June 18, 1882, the day of its grand opening. The bar boasted Denver's largest plate glass windows, which framed a garden of tropical plants. This oasis cost over ten thousand dollars with its solid marble floors, cherry tables, grand chandeliers, stained glass, and thirty-two-foot-long marble bar. In the basement rathskeller, an eleven-woman orchestra specialized in classical performances such as Haydn's *Creation*.

Such palaces bore little resemblance to the "shebang" bars of the 1860s. Rather than the Taos Lightning and "baptized" and "overnight" whiskeys (i.e., watered-down and homemade) standard in earlier bars, fashionable cafes served a wide and exotic range of domestic and foreign liquors. An international potpourri of bottled spirits fringed the backbar mirrors and overflowed into nearby mahogany display cases. Tin-lined wooden iceboxes kept beer and wine chilled.

Polished mahogany replaced the raw pine planks of Denver's puppy days. Diamond-dust mirrors and flocked wallpaper covered once bare walls, and plank seats and barrel tables evolved into posh, curtained booths. The dirt and sawdust floors where the pioneers had tossed drinks to keep down the dust were supplanted by Turkish carpets and marble floors. Bartenders hung linen towels on the bar counter and added moustache cups to their shelves so patrons could keep their beards and moustaches neat and dry.

Arnold Siebold converted his twenty-five-foot-long bar inside the Bismarck bistro into a glass-topped aquarium filled with five varieties of trout. If tipplers tired of studying the fish, they could examine the frescoes in Siebold's palatial parlor which boasted gold-tinsel and nickel-plate trim, mahogany and cherry furnishings, tile floors, and marble wainscoting.

After electric lighting became fashionable, each resort tried to outshine its competitors. Mart Watrous installed a huge electric sign in 1909 that eclipsed the old-fashioned, painted signs of his Curtis Street neighbors. Stauffer's on Welton Street used soft, tinted light shades to give a warm glow to its interior, a refinement rarely found in other recently electrified places. After installing the marvelous new light bulbs, few wanted to hide them behind shades. Electric fans were hung from tin ceilings to stir up the flies and stale air.

The Wayside Inn courted the wealthy and fashionable set by advertising itself as the mecca of motorists. "Dozens of automobiles may be seen ranged outside, in the hotel yard, and overflowing into the road," an awed reporter wrote of this display of the toys of the rich. Although an exhibit of wealth and progress in 1909, car-surrounded taverns would become a less rare and wondrous sight in future years. The Mozart Cafe downtown was headquarters for a taxi fleet of Locomobiles and Pierce Arrows. Travelers on two wheels had their resorts, too. After the Denver Wheelmen voted to keep their clubhouse dry, dissenting bicyclists could pedal to Krimminger's Bicycle Exchange Saloon.

Respectable places sought to escape the saloon stigma and to defend their virtues. "The objectionable feature of a bar in connection is eliminated," Stauffer's boasted, and "no objectionable element is tolerated."

"No promiscuous persons are allowed on the grounds," another inn advertised, adding that "men are not even allowed to invite a lady who is a stranger to them to dance." Alcoholic beverages were promoted as wholesome "food," and pictures of rosy-cheeked girls drinking beer and respectable-looking men sipping liquor were published in response to charges that alcohol poisoned body and soul. Use Zang's Liquid Foods, urged one ad; "They are appetizing, nourishing, strengthening."[29]

Despite the elegance of some saloons, the institutional image remained seamy. As brewery syndicates gained control of more bars and as saloons increasingly became confined to poorer, working-class, immigrant, and crime-plagued neighborhoods, prohibitionists found larger and friendlier audiences. But even after prohibitionists charged that saloons bred social evils, few liquor men considered reform. Instead, they turned to the political scene, where they had forged alliances with city hall from the time of the city government's beginnings. Confronted by mounting criticism, the liquor industry intensified its efforts to elect protective politicial bosses. The subsequent election frauds and political scandals provided prohibitionists with yet another charge to add to the long list of saloonhall sins.

Chapter 9
BARS AND BOSSES

On the national scene, Mark Twain, Henry Adams, and other Gilded Age commentators were focusing on the corruption of the democratic system. From Boss Tweed's New York, the search for urban corruption moved to other American cities. Intellectuals, journalists, prohibitionists, and other reformers began looking for and finding bosses, as a wide and disparate range of politicians found themselves labeled. In many cities, critics focused on the relations between city hall and saloons that generated votes for political machines.

Colorado correspondents joined the hunt and were not disappointed. In Denver, politicians and saloonists had collaborated from the beginning, from the barroom birth of both municipal and territorial government to the statehood election of 1876. Beginning in the 1880s, however, exposés of saloon politics forced one mayor to resign, drove another to abandon his reelection plans, and helped elect a reform administration that rolled out the carpet for prohibition.

Although they agreed on little else, the *Rocky Mountain News,* the *Denver Times,* the *Denver Republican,* and leading Colorado political commentators Robert Gordon Dill, David Day, and James "Fitz-Mac" McCarthy all concluded that Colorado and Denver politics were corrupt.[1] Elections were regularly followed by charges that Ed Chase and other saloonkeepers had rigged the registration, bought votes, stuffed ballot boxes, and otherwise manipulated the vote. Critics contended that politicians allowed Chase and other underworld figures to operate gambling, sporting, and drinking houses in exchange for the saloon vote.

City authorities failed to "do their duty in repressing the vicious and criminal classes," the *News* charged, "because the Republican managers have always depended upon these very classes for the often fraudulent majorities which have enabled them to remain in place and power."[2] Many Denverites may have regarded the *News,* a Democratic paper after W. A. H.

Loveland purchased it in 1878, as a biased source. But charges of collusion between the city's governing elite and the demimonde were substantiated by a court investigation of the 1889 city election. For this election, according to the *News,* liquor manufacturers, wholesalers, distributors, and retailers raised twenty thousand dollars to be distributed to "every rounder, heeler, dive keeper and tin horn gambler in town enabling them to pay for every vote cast for Wolfe Londoner."[3]

The new mayor prided himself on being a Colorado pioneer. He had run away from his Russian-Jewish family in New York City in the 1850s. His parents next heard from their eleven-year-old son when he finally wrote a letter from gold-rush San Francisco, where he was washing dishes. A few years later, the adventurous youth joined the Colorado gold rush. In 1866, Londoner gravitated to Denver, where he opened a grocery store. Two decades later, his store was said to be doing a business worth a million dollars a year, a boast in keeping with Londoner's lush walrus moustache and portly figure.

In preparation for the 1889 city election, Denver's Democrats and Prohibitionists entered a short-lived political marriage under the name of the Citizens' Ticket. Together, these unusual bedfellows sought to curb the political power of the saloon and its Republican allies. Specifically, the new party demanded a Sunday closing ordinance for tippling houses. Although Sunday closing was required by state law, city officials refused to enforce it, claiming that they had exclusive jurisdiction over drink in Denver.

To thwart the Citizens' Ticket, the liquor party went beyond the usual procedure of rigging the registration rolls with "dead names" to be used by repeaters and illegal voters. "It is known beyond question," the press declared,

> that the registration of the city is substantially under the control of saloon politics, and the canvases which have been made from house to house, ostensibly to secure a fair registration, have been in fact a means employed [to] give citizens the impressions that their names would be placed on the books, whereas in nearly every precinct the names of persons suspected of favoring Sunday closing have been excluded from registry.[4]

Election day, April 2, 1889, turned into a carnival of abuses. Reportedly because of their twenty-thousand-dollar slush fund, saloonkeepers were able to pay two dollars per vote. Bonuses for repeaters were generously awarded in the form of lottery tickets and free beers. Tramps and hoodlums from nearby towns were brought to Denver and marched to the polls by election-day special deputies. Among the illegal voters were "solid brigades marched up from the Palace and Mascot Theatres" run by Ed Chase.[5]

Evidently the army of repeaters soon exhausted the long list of "dead names," since hundreds of legitimate voters arrived at the polls only to be turned away because persons had already voted in their names. When irate citizens complained to the deputies, they were told to stop interfering with the election. Some frustrated voters were threatened with the paddy wagon and two were actually hauled off to jail. When the Citizens' party candidate for mayor, Elias Barton, complained to police chief Henry Brady, he was told to "go to hell."[6]

Gambling hall proprietors Jefferson Randolph "Soapy" Smith and William Barclay "Bat" Masterson played leading roles in the manipulation of voters. The con man and the gunman collaborated in preparing hundreds of slips containing registered "dead names" and helped distribute them to unqualified voters. "Soapy" boarded up one polling place, forcing voters to hand their ballots through planks to an unseen poll judge, who could easily discard undesirable votes.

The *News* pronounced the 1889 mayoral election to be "the most disgraceful in the history of Denver politics, corrupt as they have been before." Even the *Denver Republican* conceded that a corrupt gang had been permitted to sully the GOP campaign. After both city and county officials refused to investigate the election, Elias Barton carried his complaint to the state supreme court, which ordered the Arapahoe County Court to hear the case. Following a trial that uncovered gross voting abuses, Mayor Londoner was removed from office shortly before his term was to expire, the only mayor in Denver history to be so humiliated.[7]

Even while the trial proceeded, the questionably elected officials handed out rewards to liquor men and the city council granted tavern licenses in theretofore saloonless residential districts. Sunday closing demands were evaded by an ordinance stating that restaurants could sell liquor with Sunday meals. This law triggered a sudden explosion in the number of Denver restaurants. Saloons hastily set up lunch counters serving soup and crackers. Customers of the beer dives bought crackers for twenty-five cents and got a free mug of lager. At the Tabor Opera House tavern, a large and thirsty crowd assembled on Sundays to buy clam chowder. To help wash down the chowder, customers welcomed the complimentary three-finger shot of whiskey. "Of course," the *News* noted drily, "it is not incumbent on the patron to eat the soup and the same plate was doubtless the means of securing many drinks."[8]

Other episodes further demonstrated the Londoner administration's leniency with bars. Despite the city ordinance prohibiting saloons within five-hundred feet of any church or school, parson Thomas Uzzell of the People's Tabernacle complained that his church was surrounded by a dozen saloons, whose patrons endangered his life many times. Yet, the parson added, the police were "never around when trouble comes" although "they are always about when I give an oyster supper."[9]

Rarely did the saloon's undermining of politics arouse the public from its apathy. Only such gross fraudulence as that of the 1889 election caused a public outcry great enough to force an investigation that revealed the extent to which liquor men influenced urban politics.

After the Londoner debacle, Denverites made their first major attempt at urban reform. In the 1891 city election, which the *Denver Times* called admirable and above criticism, voters elected as their mayor a former Arapahoe County district and criminal court judge, Platt Rogers. A handsome, beardless, stern-eyed idealist, Rogers drew support from the same coalition of Democrats, suburbanites, and reformers that had hoped to install Elias Barton in City Hall.

The new administration began studying municipal ownership of the utility companies, cracked down on gambling, and earnestly strove to improve city government. Regulation of saloons was a key part of this urban reform. For the first time, boasted Mayor Rogers, the Sunday and midnight closing laws were rigidly enforced. Mayor Rogers was singled out by *Harper's Weekly* for smashing a political ring that relied on saloon politics, dishonest elections, and a corrupt police force. "Denver," *Harper's* observed, "still feels the shock of its elevation to a place among the well-governed cities of the land." While noting that the Market Street red-light district was still "notorious in the West" and the "gambling hells" still flourished, the article claimed that

> now drinking and gaming cease at midnight, under a new law that is exceptionally well enforced. Mondays had been "field days" for the trials of arrested drunkards, but the number decreased remarkably. A similar decrease of the cases of destitution was noticed. About 400 saloons pay $242,000 into the city treasury each year. The city appoints policemen to keep order in the gambling "hells" at the expense of the proprietors.[10]

Mayor Rogers' administration had some help from the state legislature in controlling alcohol. The 1889 General Assembly passed a high license law, raising the minimum saloon license fee to six-hundred-dollars. In 1891, anti-saloonists pushed through state laws closing saloons from midnight until 6:00 A.M. and all day Sunday. Furthermore, in 1893, Rogers persuaded the state legislature to approve a new city charter that provided for tavern licenses only if a majority of property owners fronting on a block petitioned for a saloon and if it was not within five hundred feet of a public school. Although the 1893 charter continued to allow the city council "exclusively to provide for licensing, taxing and regulation" of saloons, its power was curtailed by the additional stipulation that after the council acted the Fire and Police Board was to administer the license system with power to revoke council-awarded licenses. This arrangement simply added another layer of government for saloonmen to buy off with bribes and votes, and it also gave rise to the political machine of Denver's most powerful boss.[11]

Although Denver city government needed reform, the state legislature was hardly the body to undertake it. The 1889 legislature which initiated Denver government by state board was the famous "Robber Seventh," so named because of its reckless expenditures and the amount of state furniture and furnishings its members carried home with them. State solons complained about saloon influence over city government while they held official sessions in the White House Saloon. Even the state senate's committee on temperance, according to one senator, "should more properly have been called the intemperance committee as the room assigned to this committee constituted a free dispensary of many choice wines and liquors."[12] While this venal seventh general assembly claimed to be reforming the city, the desire to share in Denver's political spoils and patronage and the antiurban bias of rural legislators were probably the main motivating factors.

After the reform administrations of Platt Rogers (1891–93) and Thomas S. McMurray (1895–99), others joined *Harper's* in proclaiming Denver politically clean. "In no other city in America," exulted one minister in 1897, "does the saloon element dominate city politics so little as in Denver."[13]

He spoke too soon. Behind the scenes during the 1890s, Robert Walter Speer was building a political machine that would make him Denver's most powerful boss. Speer established relations with liquor men that would keep his machine well oiled and running smoothly. At the turn of the century, on the eve of Speer's long reign at city hall, the saloon was still very much a part of politics. A seamy picture can be drawn with considerable accuracy from testimony collected by the State Voters' League, a reform group created in 1905 by Edward P. Costigan, Judge Benjamin B. Lindsey, General Irving Hale, and other prominent citizens.

Colorado's State Voters' League was one of a succession of organizations founded during the early twentieth century to fight political corruption. It was preceded by the Honest Elections League, whose reform efforts were stymied by the state supreme court, and followed by the more successful Citizens' Party. The Colorado Voters' League, which was modeled after the Voters' League of Illinois, published the *Voters' Bulletin*, edited by William McLeod Raine (who later became a prominent Colorado novelist). After attracting little support outside of Denver, from either major party or from the press, the State Voters' League disappeared the year after its founding. But for a few months it spotlighted political corruption that many Coloradans preferred to overlook.

At the northeast corner of Larimer Street and Cherry Creek stood a stone structure with the carved entryway inscription, "City Hall." Inside, the coarse talk, tobacco smoke, and aroma of alcohol gave it the air of just another Larimer Street saloon. In the council chambers alcoholic fumes wafted about during aldermanic meetings that had become a drunken disgrace. Council chaplain Thomas Uzzell complained that President John

Conlon requested opening prayers in "a drunken and disorderly way." After lavishly bestowing liquor licenses and valuable public utility franchises, the city solons often adjourned automatically, for Conlon was "so drunk that he could not put the motion."[14]

The political scene portrayed by early-twentieth-century reformers contrasts sharply with the rosy city history completed by Jerome Smiley in 1901 and the official journal of the city launched by Mayor Speer in 1909. But if Smiley and Speer overlooked the scandals of their day, reformers interested in advancing their own causes and careers tended to overstate the role of demon rum in corrupting city hall. A hand-drawn chart of the 1905 Denver power structure in the papers of reformer Edward P. Costigan, for instance, relegated saloons to a minor position in Speer's machine.[15] Evidently not all reformers believed their own rhetoric about saloon-infested government. Yet many of them continued to link the enemies of reform and any and all municipal maladies to demon rum. If not the source of all evil, the liquor houses at least seemed to be the most plausible scapegoat.

Reformers relished pointing out that city hall was surrounded by drinking establishments. On the 1300 block of Larimer Street alone (where city hall stood) there were seven saloons. Nicolletti Brothers (1301), Henry Geise's Annex (1313), Bernstein's (1323), Gilpin Bar (1332), Circle Bar (1324), California Hall (1344), and J. J. Bond's (1362) were reinforced by Councilman Gahan's pubs at 1133 and 1401 and the Weil Brothers' large wholesale liquor emporium at 1405 Larimer.

As evidence of bar-blighted city government, antisaloon publicists also pointed to the number of tavernkeeping councilmen. During the first decade of the twentieth century, nine of Denver's sixteen wards were represented, at one time or another, by saloonkeepers. This phenomenon was by no means unique to Denver. In New York, Chicago, and across the country a favorite joke among urban reformers concerned tactics for ending city council meetings abruptly: simply have a youngster rush in yelling, "Mister! Mister! Your saloon is on fire!"

In the First Ward (the old Auraria neighborhood wedged between Cherry Creek, the South Platte River, and West Colfax Avenue) James P. Coates held the council seat from 1904 to 1913. Coates, born in Wisconsin in 1861, came to Denver in 1895 and found work as a barkeeper. Four years later, he acquired the St. Joe Hotel and tavern at 842 Larimer Street. This small hotel housed thirty-seven boarders, according to the 1900 census and, according to the Voters' League, had a maximum capacity of forty guests. Yet during the 1904 election, Coates' hotel housed ninety-six registered voters. Coates did not object to his many boarders, as their names—often of deceased or nonexistent persons—came in handy on election day (see map 6).[16]

On the east side of Cherry Creek, the Second Ward, consisting of the heart of old Denver, was represented by councilman John P. Jones. He was

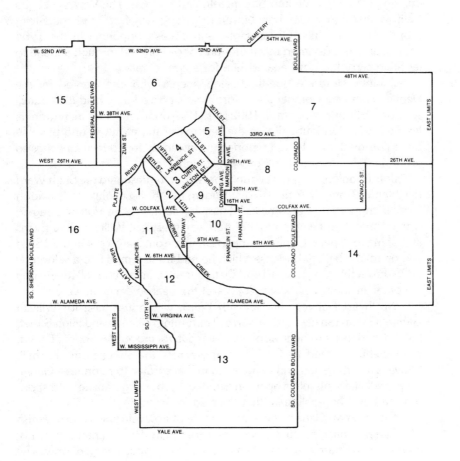

Map 6. Denver Ward Boundaries, 1900–1912

a Welshman who arrived in Denver in the early 1890s and operated various drinking halls and a Welton Street casino and saloon. The Voters' League testified that Jones was bribable and "getting rich fast." George Stein, proprietor of the Inter-Ocean Hotel and Jones's opponent in the 1904 council election, declared that Jones had once "offered through a friend to let Stein carry the ward against him for a consideration."[17]

Andrew Horan, a one-time saloonkeeper who also worked for the Denver Tramway Company and for Speer's police force, held the council seat for the Fourth Ward from 1902 to 1912. Councilman Horan, reformers testified, was "undoubtedly on the pay roll of the tramway and possibly other corporations." Horan reportedly showed up for council meetings so drunk that he could not talk or walk straight.[18]

John Conlon, long-time council president, represented the Sixth Ward (Highlands) from 1902 until 1913. Known as "Honest John" to his North Denver supporters, Conlon was "Tramway John" to the Voters' League, who claimed that he was a tool of tramway president William Gray Evans and of Mayor Speer. Conlon came to Denver from New York in the 1880s and opened a bakery business which he had transformed into a saloon by 1895. From this groggery at 1442 Platte Street, Conlon controlled an army of voters, including many employees of the nearby Zang Brewery.[19]

Northeast Denver, the Seventh Ward, was home base for William Gahan. Gahan ran his ward saloon at Thirty-ninth Avenue and High Street, but he and his brothers also maintained two groggeries, one of them conveniently located at 1401 Larimer, across the street from city hall. "Always a corporation and tramway man," according to reformers, Gahan supposedly kept his joints open on Sunday, harbored gambling, and sponsored a boys' baseball team that "played for beer."[20]

Councilman Gahan offers an example of how reformers could tarnish and Speer's machine could extol the same man. Was Gahan a pawn of corporate and tramway interests as the Voters' League charged, or was he the civic leader praised in Mayor Speer's magazine, *Municipal Facts*? In the latter source, a photograph shows Gahan to be a clean-shaven city father and the capsule biography pronounces him to be "deeply interested in and well versed in municipal affairs." His saloonkeeping is not mentioned. Gahan is said to be "in the wholesale cigar business."[21] When reformers accused Gahan of serving beer to his boys' baseball team, they meant to blacken his name. However, this charge also reveals that Gahan provided recreation for the boys of his industrial northeast Denver ward.

Councilman George Weick's Eleventh Ward consisted of the area south of West Colfax Avenue between the Platte River and Cherry Creek and north of Sixth Avenue. Weick, whose illiteracy appalled reformers, ran a tavern and meat market, drank heavily, and was notorious for changing his political position overnight. His political agility was explained by the charge that he "was commonly considered to be for sale."[22]

Denver's rednosed aldermen were part of the rubber-stamp council of Robert Walter Speer, the only man whom Denverites ever commonly called "boss." Speer looked like a boss. He stood six feet tall and came to weigh a good two hundred pounds that looked muscular rather than flabby. Desite a dome that grew as shiny as the one atop the state capitol, his skin was fresh, his jaw firm, and his eyes clear. Behind the bulldog frame, the easy smile, and the strong handshake lay a political genius of the first order.

Speer established a large following among a wide variety of voters, ranging from the barroom, blue-collar crowd to the business elite of the Denver Club. Although a Democrat, Speer convinced many leading Republicans that he could best serve their interests. His amiable relations with the opposition party paid off in 1891, when Republican governor John L. Routt appointed Speer the minority party member of the newly created Denver Fire and Police Board.

Speer used this position to build up support among both the police and the elements they policed. Using his power to review the liquor licenses granted by the city council, Speer gained a following among the saloon-keepers and associated gambling, prostitution, and vice interests. His covert alliance with underworld ace Ed Chase became rather obvious in 1899. When public clamor about Chase's policy shops (which offered lottery tickets and other gambling opportunities) became embarrassing to Speer, Chase obligingly shut them down. Shortly afterward, while Speer looked the other way, Chase's gambling operations reopened as "social clubs."

To cultivate more votes in the downtown wards, Speer inaugurated a welfare plan whereby policemen gave away coupons to indigents. The poor could then redeem the coupons at saloons for sandwiches, hard-boiled eggs,and beer.[23] Ostensibly a charitable measure, this early food-stamp program was probably designed to help both the poor and the saloonkeepers remember Speer on election day.

In 1904, after years of manipulating mayors and councilmen, Speer ran for mayor. According to the defeated Republian mayoral candidate, John W. Springer, fifteen thousand fraudulent votes were cast for Speer. A Democratic source, the anti-Speer *Denver Times,* reported that over seventeen thousand fictitious names were found in the Denver registration books. With such support, Speer defeated Springer by a healthy margin despite the opposition of all four daily papers. "It cost us more to defeat Springer," Walter S. Cheesman griped afterward, "than any other man who ever ran for office in Denver!" The seven wards controlled by saloonkeeping aldermen and councilman Weick's Eleventh Ward gave Speer the victory.[24]

Saloons poured out drinks, dollars, and votes for Speer. Proprietor Pat Hickey paid his political dues by registering and trying to force some sixty hoboes to vote. When his fraudulent voters were disqualified, Speer's henchmen assessed Hickey five-hundred-dollars in place of the votes. One divekeeper, Billy Green, supposedly delivered as many as 500 fraudulent votes from his downtown precinct. "Green County," as his Market Street domain was called, once reported 717 votes cast for the Democratic candidate and only 17 for the Republican.[25]

The new mayor did not disappoint his barroom boosters. Despite the enemies it earned him, Speer publicly defended the saloon's existence, speaking candidly in his 1904 inaugural address:

> No effort will be made to make a puritanical town out of a growing Western city. . . . You must take people as you find them, and by a firm and persistent policy, make conditions better gradually. Spasmodic and sensational efforts of reform will be avoided. Vice will not run riot, but wherever found will be properly controlled and suppressed. . . . Social evils that cannot be abolished will be restricted and regulated so as to do the least possible harm.

Again in 1909, the mayor told the Methodist Brotherhood: "The city deals with all classes. . . . It deals with classes widely different in thought and in action and in feeling. And the city is ruled by majorities. No law can be successfully enforced unless the majority believe in it. . . . What evils we have thus far been unable to rid ourselves of are at least not hidden evils. At least we are able to diagnose our case with accuracy. And that is a great deal for any city to say."[26]

Speer defended Denver's saloons not only with words but with adroit political action. He undermined the hopes of prohibitionists who placed a local-option prohibition amendment on the Denver ballot in 1910 by proposing a watered-down alternative. Speer's amendment to the city charter proposed a modest raise in the price of liquor licenses and limited their number to one per every seven hundred Denverites. By promoting this amendment as a moderate compromise and branding city-wide prohibition as a radical measure, the Speer camp coaxed Denverites to reject local option by a margin of almost two to one.

While opposing prohibition, Speer respected the moral geography advocated by the ever growing numbers of suburban voters. He helped to arrange a compromise that protected dry neighborhoods while allowing the inner city to maintain its saloons. The Speer city charter reassured suburbanites that "all laws and ordinances prohibiting or regulating the sale of spiritous, malt or intoxicating liquors in municipalities annexed to the city of Denver or, consolidated with the City and County of Denver, shall remain in force."[27]

Thus the Speer compromise gave the bedroom suburbs the saloonless status they sought, but preserved the vice, dice, and booze district. Doubtless some suburbanites found this arrangement pleasurable and lingered at the downtown end of the streetcar line after work (see maps 7 and 8). "Just

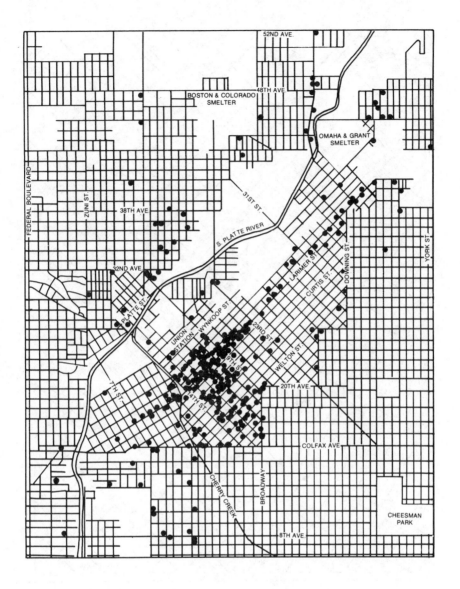

Map 7. Denver Saloons in 1915

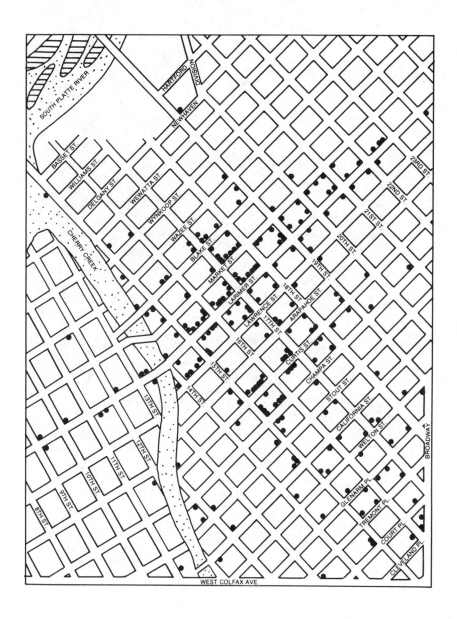

Map 8. Downtown Denver Saloons in 1915

one more" probably became a common phrase among some of the men headed home for saloonless suburbs and dry households.

Mayor Speer accommodated the suburban prohibitionists but did so without alienating urbanites who favored taverns. The downtown saloon district served immigrant and industrial city dwellers and businessmen who insisted that Denver's status as a regional metropolis, convention city, and tourist attraction depended on recreational facilities, including the taverns, gambling houses, and bordellos for which Denver had become famous. By giving liquor men, gamblers, and other downtown operators their own district, Speer also ensured their continued political loyalty and cemented his working relationship with Ed Chase. This liaison gave Speer an intelligence service and a command post in the underworld. With Chase's help, undesirable newcomers and particularly objectionable criminals, pimps, prostitutes, gamblers, and bunco artists could be identified. More importantly the Speer-Chase connection facilitated the confinement of the worst bars, the gambling halls, and prostitution to lower downtown Denver where they would be least objectionable.

Speer found Chase helpful at the polls and in managing the city, and Chase found Speer helpful in protecting his gambling and saloon interests. The mayor even arranged to make a dream come true for the lord of the underworld—veto power in the selection of Denver's district attorney. Chase's extralegal role in screening applicants for the chief criminal prosecutor's job was discovered by a young Denver attorney, Benjamin Barr Lindsey, who had worked hard for the Speer machine and asked to be considered for the district attorney's office. Lindsey was told to discuss his future with Ed Chase.

During the interview, the gambler sat quietly stroking his gray mustache, looking "a little embarrassed" and nodding occasionally while a henchman explained to Lindsey: "Mr. Chase doesn't want anything but what's fair. He doesn't expect to run wide open all the time. When the District Attorney has to make a demonstration, he's willing to pay up." Even Lindsey, Denver's most celebrated reformer, seemed overawed by the city's underworld ace. Chase, Lindsey recounted,

> was reputed to be a millionaire, and he lived then—as he does now—in considerable luxury on Capitol Hill, and associated with the most reputable business men in the community. He was greatly respected in various quarters. . . . He was also a stockholder in several utility corporations, and his influence in politics was well known. . . .
>
> Chase was an elderly man, with gray hair and moustache. He would pass anywhere as a nice, clean "office man" careful of his health and his appearance.[28]

Chase correctly judged Lindsey to be an unreliable party man. But Speer, hoping to keep Lindsey loyal, had him appointed county court judge.

In that position, Lindsey rose to international prominence as the developer and advocate of the juvenile court system. However, he also became the prime critic of the Speer machine, or the "beast," as he called it. The path of the "beast," according to Lindsey, led "from the dives to the Police Board, from the Police Board to the lower courts, from the courts to the political leaders who nominated the judges of the courts, and from the political leaders to the corporation magnates who ruled all."[29]

Judge Lindsey, a mouselike man barely five feet tall and weighing less than one hundred pounds, argued that the saloon vote had become a tool of Denver's power elite. He maintained that William G. Evans, Walter S. Cheesman, and David H. Moffat, who wanted political protection for their privately owned public utilities, relied on Chase and Speer to stave off reformers proposing increased regulation, if not public ownership, of Evans's tramway company, Cheesman's water company, and Moffat's railroads.

Lindsey's "beast" consisted of a Democratic mayor supported by a Republican power elite, an alliance which confused some Republicans, who brought suit against the Speer-Evans-Chase machine in 1904. When Chase contributed one-thousand-dollars to the Republican party, Lindsey pronounced that beast to be scratching its right ear with its left hind leg. In appreciation for Chase's "scratch," it was understood that the GOP would drop its election fraud suit.[30]

Lindsey's contention that the machine started out with the dives and reached into the highest strata of government proved valid in the case of Daniel Cronin, an operator arrested for illegally serving two women. In his court, Lindsey found Cronin guilty, a decision sustained by the state and national supreme courts. At every stage of the appeals process, the tavernkeeper had his expenses paid by the Speer machine and his case argued by the Democratic party's state chairman.[31]

If sporting houses and saloons helped elect Speer, their support also helped to undo him in 1912, for the mayor's underworld connections left him vulnerable. In 1912, opponents indicted Speer for "unlawfully, knowingly and willingly permitting certain common, ill-governed and disorderly houses, to the encouragement of idleness, gaming, drinking, fornication and other misbehavior."[32] That same year reformers launched a mayoral campaign for Henry J. Arnold, an assessor whom Speer had ousted from office in a widely publicized effort to enforce machine regularity. Speer decided not to run again, perhaps guessing that if the reformers were given their inning at bat they would strike out, for their strength and their unity consisted in little more than having a common foe—Boss Speer.

George W. Creel, the new police commissioner under Mayor Arnold, pounced on prostitution, gambling, and saloons. With the same zeal he later (as President Woodrow Wilson's public information officer) showed in attacking Germany, Creel waged war on Denver's demimonde. Saloon licensing and closing laws were rigidly enforced, as were the antigambling laws. Creel rounded up hundreds of "half-naked women [who] sat for sale beside a soiled bed and a dirty washbowl" along Market Street.[33] Although Creel's plan to rehabilitate these ladies on a municipal poor farm failed, he did disband the Market Street flesh markets. By capitalizing on the national concern about white slavery and borrowing ideas from other cities cracking down on prostitution, Creel was able to close one of the West's most notorious and well-established red-light districts. After the 1912 crackdown, Market Street became known as "Padlock Alley."

The city cleansers also tackled saloon politics, their prime target since the 1880s. They did away with the city council and saloonkeeping ward bosses by inspiring voters to approve an experiment with commission government. The new administration enforced previously passed laws prescribing a six-hundred-dollar annual saloon fee, due in advance; midnight to 6:00 A.M. and Sunday closing; restaurant liquor sale only, with a special two-hundred-dollar per annum license and only with bona fide meals; and exclusion of saloons from five of sixteen Denver wards.

The new administration refused to issue any new saloon licenses (although previously held licenses could be transferred to new establishments). The sentiments of the reformed city hall were evident in a letter from police commissioner Creel's office to a St. Joseph, Missouri, businessman who hoped to relocate in Denver: "We have 467 saloons in this city and I regret to state that a few of them are making money . . . We could not issue you a new license."[34]

The ultimate blow to saloonhall government, however, came on November 3, 1914, when Coloradans voted 129,589 to 118,017 to begin prohibition on January 1, 1916, four years ahead of national prohibition. Although Denver had voted 38,139 to 29,533 against the dry crusade, the city was forced to go along with the statewide decision.

The bars were banned and the boss evidently went straight. In 1916, Denver voters elected Speer as mayor, reinstated the strong mayor form of government, and resurrected the city council. Although the reformers were voted out, they left their mark on the city and on its boss. Speer ran a far cleaner race in 1916 than he had in 1904. Even his old political ally and new rival for the United States Senate, former governor Charles S. Thomas, pronounced the 1916 election an honest one. "Profitting from his past experiences," Thomas wrote of Speer, "[he] remained aloof from demoralizing and sinister influences." For the first time, every Denver district (reformers had replaced the old ward system with election districts) gave Speer more votes than his Republican opponent, William W. Booth. Speer survived, but the old-time saloon with all its election-day activities largely disappeared from the city's political life.[35]

Speer easily won reelection with the near-unanimous support of Denver's business community, which found reform government inefficient, unprofitable, and no fun. Puritanical purges of prostitution, gambling, and drinking houses damaged Denver's appeal as a convention and tourist city. Denver's masses also returned to Speer, after comparing his concrete improvements with the platitudes and promises of progressive city purifiers. "I am a boss," Speer once confessed, but added, "I want to be a good one."[36]

Ed Chase too had changed. Retiring from politics and vice, the white-haired octogenarian settled into a mansion at the corner of tree-lined East Colfax Avenue and Race Street. Among his neighbors on Colfax were his old adversaries, Mayor Platt Rogers and Senator Edward Costigan of the Voters' League. Few who saw the tall, dapper gentleman in goggles and dustcoat taking afternoon cruises in his Thomas Flyer recognized the long-time boss of Denver's underworld.

When the eighty-three-year-old Chase died of pneumonia on September 27, 1921, he was treated with a tinge of nostalgic fondness by the same newspapers that had condemned him during his long life. The *Rocky Mountain News* called him "a law in the lower wards," and mentioned his reputed millionaire status. Other papers divulged that the Chase estate included heavy investments in Denver utilities, notably in the old Evans family vehicle, the Denver Tramway Company, of which Chase had been one of the original incorporators. Chase was pronounced the city's gambling king, a leading promoter of the theaters, a successful real estate investor, and a respected capitalist. He was praised as a quiet, charitable person and a man true to his word. Chase "got on pretty well with all classes," noted the journal of the Society of Sons of Colorado, and "ultimately came to be a power in politics [who] was consulted by most of the 'bosses.' "[37]

One of Chase's gambling and saloon business associates, Vaso Chucovitch, had replaced him as underworld czar before the gambler cashed in his chips. A hefty, red-mustachioed Slav, Chucovitch had courted Speer and taken Chase's place as the broker between the bars and the boss. It was the effusive Chucovitch, not the secretive Chase, who left a monument to Denver's preprohibition saloon politics. On his death in 1933, Chucovitch willed one-hundred-thousand-dollars for a civic center monument to Speer, who had died in office in 1918. Such an obvious tribute to the boss from the city's leading gambler and divekeeper, however, would never do. Municipal officials reshuffled Chucovitch's cash to pay for a children's wing for Denver General Hospital. Reformers must have breathed easier. A saloonkeeper's tribute to Denver's best-known mayor might have perpetuated a political past that many hoped would be forgotten.[38]

The alliance between political bosses and liquor men, designed to ensure their survival, came to endanger both. Confronted by the pressure politics of prohibitionists and other reformers, even the most powerful bosses could no longer protect the saloon.

SALOON AND BAKERY.

The Immigrant Saloon

Two out of every three preprohibition saloonkeepers in Denver were foreign-born. Many of them perpetuated the social and cultural customs as well as the food and drink of their homelands.

Florian Spalti, who came from Switzerland to Denver as a wood and coal hauler in 1859, saved enough to open up a saloon at 1700 Blake Street. Spalti (right foreground in the photograph above) decorated his inn with Swiss and American flags and helped found the Swiss society that met at his place. Spalti gradually expanded his business to include a bakery, grocery, fuel company, hotel, and insurance and real estate agencies. Over the years he encouraged many of his countrymen to immigrate to Colorado, "the Switzerland of America."

One-third of the Mile-High City's taverns were operated by Germans. Charles E. Leichsenring from Saxony operated various beer halls with his sons, including this well stocked turn-of-

the century thirst and cigar parlor at 1527 Curtis Street.

Theodore Zietz of Essen brought a wife and fifteen children to Denver. His son, Henry, Sr., and grandson, Henry, Jr. (the two men in the photograph above), continued to run the family saloon he established in 1871. "My grandfather," Henry H. Zietz, Jr., reported proudly in 1973, "brought this bar from Germany in 1857." The white oak

front and back bar, large collecion of stuffed animals, and Colorado liquor license number one remain in the Buckhorn Exchange Restaurant, a designated Denver landmark still serving liquor, buffalo meat, and Rocky Mountain oysters.

THE BANK

WM. SCHAAF, Eigenthuemer

Ein gutes frisches Glass Bier und feiner Lunch den ganzen Tag. Die besten Weine, Liköre und Cigarren. Wir verkaufen den besten Whiskey in kleineren und grösseren Quantitäten.

Safe Deposit Boxes $3.00 pro Jahr

Ecke 15. und Market Str.   Denver, Colo.

TELEPHONE MAIN 3038

Cecilia Burkhardt Collection

As the most populous, prominent, and prosperous immigrant group in the city, Germans published various newspapers with advertisements such as this 1914 one for William Schaaf's Bank Saloon. Besides safety deposit boxes, the Bank also loaned and kept money for regular customers.

Dennis Gallagher Collection

Although the Irish-born represented only 3 percent of Denver's population in 1900, they operated 10 percent of the city's saloons that year. Eugene Madden (with moustache behind bar in the photograph above) conducted a saloon at 1140 Larimer Street for forty years. Simultaneously he served nine consecutive terms on the Denver City Council. Madden's Wet Goods—as neighbors dubbed it—was one of several dozen saloons used as a political center. As in New York, Chicago, and other cities, Denver's saloons became bastions of ward politics.

CHRISTOPHER COLUMBUS HALL,

A CHOICE LINE OF

Wines, Liquors and Cigars,

ALSO DEALER IN

Imported Maccaroni, Cheese and Olive Oils.

2219 Larimer Street,

DENVER,   -   -   COLORADO.

I drink at Christopher Columbus Hall.

SIRO MANGINI, Prop.

I don't, but will.

Addah Mangini Joy Collection

Italians, brought to Denver to work on the railroads, often left that dangerous, poor-paying work to open hostelries. Siro Mangini's Christopher Columbus Hall (below) opened in the 1870s as a haven for Italians, one of the poorest and least popular immigrant groups. Renamed El Bronco by new Mexican American managers in the 1960s, it is probably the oldest operating bar in Denver today.

Addah Mangini Joy Collection

Immigrant saloons were a favorite target of the Anti-Saloon League, Women's Christian Temperance Union, and the Prohibition Party. Reverend Edwin A. McLaughlin, superintendent of the Colorado Anti-Saloon League, admonished Coloradans to give "their prayers, votes and money to fight the Un-American saloon." Immigrant barkeepers often responded by draping their saloons with American flags and offering a free drink to anyone turning in antisaloon propaganda.

Chapter 10
SHUTTING THE SALOON DOOR

Saloon doors swung shut on New Year's Day, 1916. Although the buildings soon reopened as pool halls, soda shops, restaurants, candy stores, soft-drink parlors, and speakeasies, the saloon as a major social, political, and economic institution was closed for good. The bars, cocktail lounges, and nightclubs that opened after prohibition was repealed in 1933 bore little resemblance to the old-time saloon.

Saloonkeepers and their patrons were stunned in 1916, not comprehending the still-puzzling change in public attitudes that brought about the "noble experiment." Before 1914, few Colorado rednoses took the bluenoses seriously. At least, many of them failed to change their taverns to accommodate mounting public criticism. As one of the oldest and most tradition-bound of institutions, the tavern seemed incapable of restructuring itself. Of course, few drinking men felt that change was either necessary or desirable. Had not Americans, as they moved from eastern towns to western mining camps, always depended on taverns as centers of social, political, and economic activity? Yet, after centuries of tavern going in Europe and America, drinkers suddenly found themselves saloonless, victims of American idealism, progressive hopes for a better society, and widespread prejudice against the sorts of people who patronized bars.

Drinkers weakened their cause by not taking their opponents seriously enough. For years saloonkeepers simply scoffed at the cold-water coalition of the Templars, the Woman's Christian Temperance Union, the Prohibition party, and the Anti-Saloon League. Bartenders traded free drinks for temperance pledge cards which they posted on their backbars as trophies. Bibbers scoffed at Carry Nation, who was jailed in Denver for disturbing the peace and inciting a riot. Afterward, barkeepers concocted Carry Nation cocktails.

Belatedly, drinking men realized their error in not organizing more effectively against woman suffrage. In 1893, Colorado became the second

111

state to give women the vote, partly because Colorado liquor men, unlike their brethren elsewhere, failed to raise enough money and consolidate enough power to stop the suffragettes. "It was a great mistake to give women the ballot," a spokesman for Denver's saloonkeepers told the *Rocky Mountain News* on August 3, 1896, "and now that it has been granted saloon men had better look out or Colorado will be a prohibition state."

Ladies of the WCTU worked night and day to that end. They stationed themselves at saloon doors to record who entered, how long they stayed, and their condition when they left. Some bars retaliated by posting their own guards at the window to watch the saloon watchers. If the lady tried to enter, customers chanted in unison, "Whore!"[1]

Saloon men also failed to respond effectively to criticism from church people. Mounting opposition from Protestant churches might have been mollified by reform of the worst abuses. Instead, liquor men tended to react like one Larimer Street tavernkeeper. Finding a horse-drawn gospel wagon full of repentant sinners singing praises to the Lord in front of his beer parlor, he turned a hose on the wagon to drown out the evangelists. Then he asked the singers and spectators in for a drink on the house. No one accepted, gospel-wagon worker Rachel Wild Peterson proudly reported, declaring that "the Christian people of our country are used to water." Not only evangelists but more orthodox churchmen as well moved into the saloon district to combat demon rum. Reverend Henry Martyn Hart of St. John's Episcopal Cathedral established "Dean Hart's Boozeless Bar" at 1742 Lawrence Street to provide an alternative to the "devil's broth."[2]

Churchmen combatted saloon spirits with their own spirituality, perhaps aware of an idea that William James articulated: "The sway of alcohol over mankind is unquestionably due to its power to stimulate the mystical faculties of human nature, usually crushed to the earth by the cold facts and dry criticisms of the sober hour."[3]

Alcohol, ministers thundered, was a false religion and demon rum was the antichrist. Local prohibitionists brought in national prohibition speakers, including the evangelist Billy Sunday, who taught an auditorium full of Denverites to sing "The Brewer's Big White Horses Can't Run Over Me."

Churchgoers worked harder knowing that houses of alcohol outnumbered the houses of God. In a town of two hundred thousand, Denver's Ellis Meredith wrote to the WCTU's *Union Signal,* there were one hundred churches and four hundred saloons. Churches were open a total of 26,000 hours per year, while saloons were open 3,5404,000 hours a year. Thus it would take thirty-four churches, she calculated, to offset one saloon's influence. The *Union Signal's* message was clear. The godly had to be much more aggressive to defeat their numerically superior enemy. And they were. The WCTU even had Cradle Rolls for newborn infants and a Little Temperance League (L.T.L.) which taught children to sing:

C-O-L-O-Ra-DO Yell
Who are we? The L.T.L.
HO! HO! HO! Watch us Grow!
When we vote saloons will go![4]

Dry crusaders not only preached against demon rum, they also built alternative institutions to coax tipplers away from the devil's broth. Various groups established reading rooms, game halls, public restrooms, and water fountains to accommodate the bored, the tired, the thirsty, and those in need of toilet rooms. One drinking fountain, according to a national authority, was the means of closing two adjacent saloons.[5] Communities were also urged to provide large, cheerful restrooms with easy chairs and couches as well as water and toilet conveniences for the public. Denver did just that in the early twentieth century, sprinkling parks, public facilities, and fountains about the city.

As Denver became a metropolis, numerous other institutions appeared, providing services and goods once dispensed by the multifunctional saloon. During the early years, Denverites had gone to church, carried on business, cared for the sick and needy, found their housing and their women, and enjoyed social, cultural, and recreational activities in saloons. But as the "shebang city" grew up, the population began spending less time in saloons and more in other institutions. Religious congregations, to their great relief, moved out of barrooms and into their own church buildings. Banks and other business buildings replaced bars as entrepreneurial centers. Hospitals and a few welfare institutions were built. Private homes, apartments, and hotels relieved the housing shortage that had left many pioneers sleeping in saloons. Formal theaters and museums replaced taverns as cultural meccas. Libraries were built and their supporters scoffed at the claims of saloons to be "reading rooms." Edison slot machines in penny arcades, nickelodeons, and ultimately movies (first shown in Denver in 1897) attracted entertainment seekers who might otherwise drift into bars.

As the social significance of the saloon waned, its economic importance was also questioned. Liquor manufacturers, distributors, and retailers had always maintained that their business was basic to the economy, providing thousands of jobs, attracting visitors, and supporting government through liquor licenses and taxes. Antisaloon spokesmen, however, began arguing that the liquor business ruined more working men than it supported and even suggested that an end to drink would mean an end to poverty.

When workers met in saloons to organize and to hold union meetings, critics blamed drink and their saloonhall meeting places, not wretched conditions, for labor unrest. Liquor men contended that license fees and liquor taxes supported local government, and prohibitionists countered that such government income did not provide even enough to police, prosecute, and penalize saloon-bred crime. As for the tourist and business life supposedly dependent on liberal drinking and gaming laws and active nightlife, reformers claimed that barroom violence and crime actually frightened visitors away from Denver. For every economic argument in favor of alcohol, opponents came up with counterarguments.

For centuries the saloon had been accepted as an inevitable institution, for better or for worse. Then prohibitionists, influenced by the progressive idea that society could be perfected by changing the social environment, insisted that it could and should be abolished. Prohibition, Americans were promised, would end not only drunkenness, but also vice, crime, and other social ills. It would also be a means of socially controlling the "dangerous classes,"—the workers, the poor, and the minorities—who sometimes questioned the established capitalist order.

Demographic changes also diminished the importance of the saloon. Young, single males predominated in the fledgling community of the 1860s, and they used saloons as their social centers and often as their living quarters. By 1900, however, women slightly outnumbered men in the Queen City and families owning or renting their homes constituted much of the citizenry. If these families drank, they usually did so in private homes and clubs.

The nature of Denver's twentieth-century neighborhoods further cut into tavern patronage. In a few neighborhoods—Irish Auraria, Italian North Denver, Slavic Globeville, and the Jewish West Side—recently arrived immigrants lived in poor, frontierlike conditions and relied on saloons for a wide range of goods, services, and activities. Yet in the middle- and upper-class neighborhoods that housed most of the city's population by 1900, there was little, if any, need for public liquor houses. These suburbs expanded after 1900 while the once dominant, core-city neighborhoods declined as residential areas. Between 1900 and 1915, the eight central wards grew slowly or lost population while the eight peripheral wards doubled their population. In a geographical as well as an institutional sense, the city had outgrown the saloon.

The expanded size of suburban lots and houses facilitated socialization in upper-class homes that was less feasible in the smaller dwellings and row houses built on Denver's original twenty-five-foot-wide lots. Occupants of cramped, older homes with their tiny parlors and backyards welcomed an escape to the corner pub. Suburbanites, on the other hand, entertained in their spacious living rooms, on their large front porches, and in their backyards. As the genteel increasingly did their sipping in private homes or clubs, saloons were abandoned to renting and clubless classes.

Still another change, the shift of the majority of Denver's work force from blue-collar to white-collar occupations, further reduced patronage of bars. Sons of miners, railroad laborers, smelter men, and factory workers commonly went into business, government service, or the professions. And they sought a new lifestyle. These new white-collar men and their families considered the old saloons of the industrial city beneath them.

Nativists strengthened the dry crusade by stereotyping the saloon as a foreign institution. Over half of Denver's preprohibition saloonkeepers were born abroad, but most of them had been in the United States for a decade or two before coming to Denver. Many spoke English and were naturalized citizens. Yet nativists persisted in equating beer with Germans, whiskey with the Irish, wine with Italians, and tavernizing in general with anyone who looked, spoke, or acted foreign. Prohibitionists seemed blind to the fact that American-born Protestants also patronized bars. The superintendent of the Colorado Anti-Saloon League, Reverend Edwin A. McLaughlin, referred to his membership as "the organized army of consecrated men and women in Colorado who are giving their prayers, votes and money to fight the Un-American Saloon."[6] Xenophobic fears that led Coloradans to join the American Protective Association in the 1890s and the Ku Klux Klan in the 1920s in record numbers also led them to vote Colorado dry in 1914, six years ahead of national prohibition.

The change in public attitude was the greatest threat to the saloon. With the rise of specialized, sophisticated social institutions in the burgeoning capital city of Colorado, the tavern's social, political, and economic importance declined. Many citizens began to doubt that beer and whiskey joints had any beneficial purpose. In the minds of many, liquor houses had become a civic embarrassment, if not a disgrace. If Denver were indeed to become the city beautiful, the city pure and populous, that boosters and progressives envisioned, the saloon must go.

Thus a stronghold of nineteenth-century society came to be banned as antisocial. An institution that brought politics into the neighborhood tavern came to be condemned as undemocratic. And an economic enterprise that offered employment and opportunity was scrapped as wasteful of human resources. So strong was the stigma that even after repeal in 1934, the word *saloon* was outlawed by the Colorado General Assembly as a name for public drinking places.[7] (Ironically, the word *saloon* had come into nineteenth-century usage to connote the elegance and sophistication of French salons because of the increasingly seamy implications of such eighteenth-century terms as *tavern, taproom,* and *grog shop.*) Vivid memories of the saloon's influence on voters led the framers of Colorado's 1935 liquor code to order saloons closed on election day until the polls closed—a law still in effect.

Critics outlawed the word and the business and they also overlooked the saloon's significance in municipal history. Many journalists and historians had joined reformers in exaggerating and damning the institution. Once bars were banished from the city, however, they preferred to downplay the role of the saloon while emphasizing the role of other institutions such as the schools, government, dry businesses, and churches. An-

Table 5
Numerical Comparison of Selected
Denver Institutions, 1859–1920

Year	Population	Churches	Schools	Hospitals	Libraries	Banks	Saloons
1859	. . . .	0	0	0	0	0	31
1860	4,749	2	2	2	0	2	35
1870	4,759	6	4	2	1	3	48
1880	35,629	27	15	3	3	7	98
1890	106,713	81	46	9	6	16	319
1900	133,859	149	80	8	9	11	334
1910	213,381	196	103	9	11	21	410
1920	256,381	267	128	15	15	34	0

Sources: Institutions listed here are those that could afford their own physical housing (e.g., churches, not congregations, are listed). Although an institution may have existed previously, it is not included unless it had physical existence sometime during the census year. It must be remembered that these numbers are not exact, only the best approximation from sources available to me. The population is from the federal census. The other figures are largely drawn from city directories. Since city directories were not available for 1860 and 1870, the far-from-satisfactory guides of 1859, 1861, and 1871 were used in conjunction with Jerome Smiley's definitive *History of Denver* and data from newspapers and the manuscript census to fill in the gap with approximate data. The zero listing for 1920 saloons overlooks, of course, the existence of illegal speakeasies which carried on some of the saloon functions. The number of saloons for 1859, 1860, and 1870 are estimates based on available sources. The number of saloons from 1880 to 1920 are based on the city directory listings for those years.

tisaloonists, in their ardor, not only abolished the saloon but also dismissed its historical significance as the most common and functional institution to nourish the camp at the confluence that became the regional metropolis of the Rocky Mountain West. They regarded the saloon as an embarrassing, if not evil, frontier legacy.

Denver's saloons per capita had declined by 1915. According to the federal Census Bureau's *General Statistics of Cities* in 1915, the Mile-High City's 496 saloons per capita was near the national average. Although Denver had more saloons per capita than Chicago, Houston, New Orleans, and San Francisco, it had fewer than Minneapolis, New York, Omaha, and Seattle. When Coloradans voted to dehydrate the nation's highest state— Oregon, Virginia, and Washington also voted for statewide prohibition that year—they were not reacting to a local phenomenon but joining a well-organized national crusade.[8]

In fact, the saloon was neither western nor eastern but an institution primarily serving the urban poor as well as the frontier poor. Both groups lacked access to a full range of institutions and the comfortable homes and domestic refinements of the settled upper and middle classes who had little use for the saloon.

Reputable society had complained about the saloon from the very beginning in Denver. Only after the turn of the century, however, did the national climate of reform, the rise of the middle class, and the emergence of other institutions narrow the role of the saloon and enable critics to finally shut its doors.

NOTES

Chapter 1

1. Lavinia [Honeyman] Porter, "By Ox Team to California: A Narrative of Crossing the Plains in 1860," Manuscript Collections, Bancroft Library, University of California, Berkeley.

2. John D. Young, *John D. Young and the Colorado Gold Rush,* ed. Dwight L. Smith (Chicago: R. R. Donnelley and Sons, 1969), p. 20.

3. Louis L. Simonin, *The Rocky Mountain West in 1867,* translated by Wilson O. Clough (Lincoln: University of Nebraska Press, 1966), pp. 41–42.

4. Richard B. Townshend, *A Tenderfoot in Colorado* (London: Butler and Tanner, 1903), pp. 55—56, 61—64.

5. Tour of Four Mile House with curator Charles H. Woolley and Louisa Ward Arps; D. W. Working, "History of the Four Mile House," *Colorado Magazine* 18 (November 1941); 209–13; Bette D. Peters, *Denver's Four Mile House* (Denver: Golden Bell Press, 1980).

6. Letter of Mrs. Samuel Dolman to the *Trail* 17 (January 1925): 11–13.

7. *Rocky Mountain News,* November 6, 1862.

8. Junius E. Wharton and David O. Wilhelm, *History of the City of Denver* (Denver: Byers and Dailey, 1866), pp. 13–16; Louie Croft Boyd, "Katrina Wolf Murat, the Pioneer," *Colorado Magazine* 16 (September 1939): 180.

9. Howard L. Conard, *Uncle Dick Wootton: The Pioneer Frontiersman of the Rocky Mountain Region* (Chicago: R. R. Donnelley and Sons, 1957), p. 369.

10. Jerome C. Smiley, *History of Denver* (Denver: Times-Sun Publishing Co., 1901), pp. 247, 252; Wharton and Wilhelm, *City of Denver,* pp. 16–17; Diorama of Denver in 1860, Colorado Heritage Center, Denver.

11. George E. Hyde, *A Life of George Bent, Written from His Letters* (Norman: University of Oklahoma Press, 1967), p. 106.

12. Edward Chase, "The Sporting Side of Denver," an interview with Thomas F. Dawson, July 11, 1921, State Historical Society of Colorado, Denver, p. 4.

13. Record Group 21, "Records of the United States District Courts," United States District Court for Colorado, Civil Case Files, 1880, Case 483, *Richard E. Whitsitt vs. Union Depot Railroad Company et al.;* Smiley, *History of Denver,* pp. 245–46; William H. H. Larimer, *Reminiscences of General William Larimer and of*

His Son, William H. H. Larimer, Two of the Founders of Denver, comp. Herman S. Davis (Lancaster, Pa.: New Era Printing Co., 1918), pp. 106, 174, Hyde, *A Life of George Bent,* p. 106.

14. *Rocky Mountain News,* May 22, 1867.

15. *The Charter and Ordinances of the City of Denver* (Denver: Denver Publishing House, 1878), p. 191; *Compiled Ordinances and Charter: The City of Denver* (Denver: Smith-Brooks Printing Co., 1898), p. 237.

16. Simonin, *Rocky Mountain West,* p. 33.

17. Henry P. Walker, "The Rise and Decline of High Plains Freighting, 1822–1880" (Ph.D. diss., University of Colorado, 1965), pp. 308–9.

Chapter 2

1. Albert D. Richardson, *Beyond the Mississippi* (Hartford, Conn.: American Publishing Co., 1867), p. 177.

2. Horace Greeley, *An Overland Journey,* ed. Charles T. Duncan (New York: Alfred A. Knopf, 1964), pp. 136.

3. Ibid., p. 133.

4. Richardson, *Beyond the Mississippi,* pp. 278–79; William Hepworth Dixon, cited in Robert G. Athearn, *Westward the Briton* (New York: Charles Scribner's Sons, 1953), p. 39; Libeus Barney, *Letters of the Pike's Peak Gold Rush* (San Jose, Calif.: Talisman Press, 1959), p. 40.

5. Smiley, *History of Denver,* p. 370.

6. *Western Mountaineer,* December 7, 1859; *Rocky Mountain News,* October 25, 1865.

7. Barney, *Letters,* p. 50; Libeus Barney Papers, State Historical Society of Colorado Library, Denver; Smiley, *History of Denver,* pp. 335–36, 723; Louisa Ward Arps, ed., *Faith on the Frontier* (Denver: Colorado Council of Churches, 1976), p. 14.

8. Smiley, *History of Denver,* pp. 719–20.

9. Ibid., pp. 725, 342–43, 349; Wharton and Wilhelm, *City of Denver,* pp. 83, 91. Whether violence was more common on the frontier than in eastern cities is a still debated question. Richard Maxwell Brown's "The American Vigilante Tradition" in *The History of Violence in America* (New York: New York Times Books, 1969) and his *Strain of Violence* (New York: Oxford University Press, 1975) finds that vigilante actions were almost twice as common and over twice as homicidal in the West. A quantitative comparison of crimes, which could be done with census data, remains to be done, as far as I could determine.

10. Alice Polk Hill, *Tales of the Colorado Pioneers* (Denver: Pierson and Gardner, 1884), p. 64.

11. *Rocky Mountain Presbyterian,* July 22, 1874.

12. Conard, *Uncle Dick Wootton,* pp. 358–59.

13. Samuel S. Wallihan and T. O. Bigney, compilers, *The Rocky Mountain Directory and Colorado Gazeteer for 1871* (Denver: S. S. Wallihan and Co., 1870), between pp. 288–89.

14. *Rocky Mountain News,* April 7, 1870; *Trail* 6 (November 1912), back cover.

15. *The Charter and Ordinances of the City of Denver* (Denver: Byers & Dailey, 1866), p. 85; *Laws Passed at the First Session of the General Assembly of the State of Colorado* (Denver, 1877), p. 883.

16. *Rocky Mountain News,* September 29, 1879.

17. Elliot West, in his *The Saloon on the Rocky Mountain Mining Frontier* (Lincoln: University of Nebraska Press, 1979), app. A, p. 152, finds fewer saloon-keepers (41 percent) married than the general population (46.7 percent). In my investigation of the 1860 Denver federal manuscript census figures, I found that a dozen out of thirty-five saloonkeepers were married in a town where there were almost seven men for every woman.

18. Wharton and Wilhelm, *City of Denver,* p. 46.

19. Conard, *Uncle Dick Wootton,* pp. 367–68.

20. Wharton and Wilhelm, *City of Denver,* p. 92; Wallihan and Bigley, *Directory and Gazeteer,* pp. 256–57; *Rocky Mountain News,* October 12, 1865.

21. *Colorado Tribune,* February 19, 1868; *Rocky Mountain News,* August 2 and February 27, 1866; November 11 and December 16, 1868.

22. Barney, *Letters,* p. 50; Smiley, *History of Denver,* p. 906.

23. Melvin Schoberlin, *From Candles to Footlights: A Biography of the Pike's Peak Theatre, 1859–1876* (Denver: Old West Publishing Co., 1941), pp. 265–71; Joseph E. Smith, "Personal Recollections of Early Denver," *Colorado Magazine* 20 (January 1943): 14.

24. William H. H. Larimer, *Reminiscences,* pp. 183–84.

25. *Rocky Mountain News,* August 27, 1864, and October 27, 1868; *Denver Daily Gazette,* January 1, 1868.

26. Smiley, *History of Denver,* p. 457.

27. *Denver Tribune,* August 17, 1872; *Rocky Mountain News,* June 8, 1866.

28. Wharton and Wilhelm, *City of Denver,* p. 92; *Rocky Mountain News,* July 14, 1872.

Chapter 3

1. Isabella Bird, *A Lady's Life in the Rocky Mountains* (Norman: University of Oklahoma Press, 1960), pp. 137–39; 182.

2. Letter from Reverend A. T. Rankin to Mrs. Kelley, August 10, 1860, Rankin Diary, Western History Department, Denver Public Library.

3. *Rocky Mountain News,* December 26, 1865.

4. Ibid., February 2, 1875.

5. Ibid., September 18, 1867; Robert L. Perkin, *The First Hundred Years: An Informal History of Denver and the Rocky Mountain News* (Garden City, N.Y.: Doubleday and Co., 1959), p. 79.

6. Frederick Jackson Turner, "Contributions of the West to American Democracy," in Ray A. Billington, ed., *Frontier and Section* (Englewood Cliffs, N.J.: Prentice-Hall, 1961), p. 97, contends that "best of all, the West gave, not only to the American, but to the unhappy and oppressed of all lands, a vision of hope, and assurance that the world held . . . the opportunity to grow to the full measure of capacity." More recently, Daniel J. Boorstin, in *The Americans: The National Experience* (New York: Random House, 1965) says that the masculine, egalitarian

frontier ended with the arrival of women who "along with their morality . . . brought inequality" (p. 92). Robert L. Brown, in *Saloons of the American West* (Silverton, Colo.: Sundance Books, 1978) claims "the prevailing spirit of equality among all men was another widely recognized characteristic of the saloon" (p. 15). Ann Burk in "The Mining Camp Saloon as a Social Center," *Red River Valley Historical Review* 2 (Fall 1975): 386–87, concludes, "Social, educational, and financial inequalities were ignored in this environment. . . . As a frontier social club the saloon therefore was a significant influence in the melting pot and democratic equalization of the West." Richard Erdoes, in *Saloons of the Old West* (New York: Alfred A. Knopf, 1979), p. 20, contends that "class consciousness . . . lingered less and less the farther west one went. When the Alleghenies barrier finally burst and taprooms became saloons, it vanished altogether." Richard C. Wade, in *The Urban Frontier: Pioneer Life in Early Pittsburgh, Cincinnati, Lexington, Louisville, and St. Louis* (Cambridge, Mass.: Harvard University Press, 1959), and Duane A. Smith, in *Rocky Mountain Mining Camps: The Urban Frontier* (Bloomington: Indiana University Press, 1967), on the other hand, have emphasized how new western towns borrowed heavily from established eastern cities, including their discriminatory class systems. For an exploration of social conflict within the dominant white race of frontier towns, see Robert R. Dykstra, *The Cattle Towns* (New York: Alfred A. Knopf, 1968).

7. Smiley, *History of Denver*, p. 336.

8. See discussion of "bummers" in Smiley, ibid., pp. 341–42; Wharton and Wilhelm, *City of Denver*, pp. 47–48; William B. Vickers, *History of the City of Denver* (Chicago: O. L. Baskin and Co., 1880), pp. 193–95.

9. Vickers, *City of Denver*, p. 224; Alice Polk Hill, *Colorado Pioneers in Picture and Story* (Denver: Brock-Haffner Press, 1915), pp. 156–64, and David F. Halaas, *Fairmount and Historic Colorado* (Denver: Fairmount Cemetery Association, 1976), pp. 102–3. Aunt Clara Brown, a black woman inducted by the Society of Pioneers, is a notable exception, although her grave remains in Riverside's pauper section.

10. Harry E. Kelsey, Jr., *Frontier Capitalist: The Life of John Evans* (Denver: State Historical Society of Colorado, 1969), p. 121; Simonin, *The Rocky Mountain West*, p. 38.

11. Larimer, *Reminiscences*, p. 98. I visited London's Guildhall Library but was unable to find any McGaa listed as a mayor in the *City of London Directory and Livery Company Guide*. Nor could I find any mention of a castle or estate named Glenarm in the definitive *Bartholomew Gazetteer of Britain*.

12. Material from this paragraph, and the following two paragraphs, is from John White, *Sketches from America* (London: Sampson, Low, Son and Marston, 1870), p. 318.

13. Chase interview, "The Sporting Side of Denver," p. 3.

14. Smiley, *History of Denver*, p. 241; Oscar O. Winther, *The Transportation Frontier: Trans-Mississippi West, 1865–1890* (New York: Holt, Rinehart, and Winston, 1964), p. 109.

15. Chase interview, "The Sporting Side of Denver," p. 4.

16. Libeus Barney, *Letters*, p. 59.

17. This observation is based on a survey of the 1860 federal manuscript

census for Denver. See also Ralph Mann's *After the Gold Rush,* an unpublished manuscript based on his computerized Stanford University dissertation, an analysis of the social structure of two California mining towns.

18. Smiley, *History of Denver,* p. 343; *Denver Daily Gazette,* October 13, 1868.

19. The Sam Howe Scrapbooks, vol. 4 (1886), State Historical Society of Colorado, Denver, contain numerous clippings about the Green case, from which I have drawn this account.

20. *Rocky Mountain News,* September 2, 1895.

21. *Colorado Territorial Council Journal, 1870,* pp. 21–22, cited in Stephen J. Leonard, "Denver's Foreign Born Immigrants, 1859–1900" (Ph.D. diss., Claremont College, 1971), p. 175.

22. *Times* (London), November 19, 1880, cited in Roy T. Wortman, "Denver's Anti-Chinese Riot, 1880," *Colorado Magazine* 42 (Fall 1965): 283.

23. *Rocky Mountain News,* November 1, 1888; Wortman, "Denver's Anti-Chinese Riot," p. 289.

24. *Rocky Mountain News,* March 28, 1880.

25. *Denver Revised Municipal Code, 1881* (Denver, 1881), ordinance 15.

26. *Rocky Mountain News,* July 19, 1870.

27. Ibid., April 22, 1871; June 8, 1872; and July 18, 1880.

28. Ibid., February 3, 1875.

29. Bernard Rosen, "Poverty and Social Welfare in Denver, 1858–1900" (Ph.D. diss., University of Colorado, 1976), p. 271.

30. "Turnstile Town" is the title of pt. 1 of Lyle W. Dorsett's *The Queen City: A History of Denver* (Boulder, Colo.: Pruett Publishing Co., 1977); *Denver Republican,* January 1, 1909. For more data on geographical mobility, see Robert M. Tank, "Mobility and Occupational Structure on the Late Nineteenth-Century Urban Frontier: The Case of Denver, Colorado," *Pacific Historical Review* 47 (May 1978): 89–216.

31. Robert G. Athearn, *Rebel of the Rockies: The Denver and Rio Grande Western Railroad* (New Haven: Yale University Press, 1962), p. 102; Bird, *A Lady's Life,* p. 139.

Chapter 4

1. Elliott West, "Dry Crusade: The Prohibition Movement in Colorado, 1858–1933" (Ph.D. diss., University of Colorado, 1971), p. 220; *Cervi's Rocky Mountain Journal,* January 30, 1974.

2. J. J. Thomas, "In the Days of the Overland Trail," *Trail* 2 (May 1910): 6–7.

3. LeRoy R. and Ann Hafen, eds., *Reports from Colorado: The Wildman Letters, 1858–1865* (Glendale, Calif.: Arthur H. Clark Co., 1961), p. 290.

4. Smiley, *History of Denver,* p. 347.

5. West, *The Saloon on the Rocky Mountain Mining Frontier,* p. 115.

6. *The City Charter of Denver* (Denver: News Printing Co., 1862), p. 17; *The Charter and Ordinances of the City of Denver* (1866), pp. 84–85; *Rocky Mountain News,* March 14, 1875; Clyde L. King, *History of the Government of Denver* (Denver: Fisher Book Co., 1911), p. 185n.

7. Smiley, *History of Denver,* pp. 320–21; *Rocky Mountain News,* June 8, 1866; *Laws Passed at the Seventh Session of the General Assembly of the State of Colorado* (Denver: Collier and Cleveland Lithographing Co., 1889), p. 126.

8. "Proceedings of the Denver City Council," October 3, 1860, p. 36, State Historical Society of Colorado, Denver.

9. *Rocky Mountain News,* February 2, 1918; July 1, 1885; and December 16, 1897.

10. *Laws Passed at the Seventh Session,* pp. 404–5.

11. The U.S. Supreme Court upheld government regulation of the saloon as "essential to the safety, health, peace, good order and morals of the community" in the 1890 case, *Crowley v. Christiansen* (137 U.S. 86). Later, the Colorado Supreme Court came to a similar conclusion in *Schwartz v. People* (46 Colo. 239) allowing saloons to "be regulated, or entirely suppressed, through the police power of the state, in the interests of good government, clean morals, and the general welfare."

12. Young, *John D. Young,* p. 55; Richardson, *Beyond the Mississippi,* p. 188.

13. *Session Laws of Colorado Territory* (Central City: David C. Collier, 1866), p. 59; King, *Government of Denver,* p. 53.

14. Unless otherwise noted, my account of Chase and quotes from him are from the Chase interview, "The Sporting Side of Denver."

15. Schoberlin, *From Candles to Footlights,* p. 219.

16. U.S. Census Bureau, Manuscript Census for Denver City, Arapahoe County, Colorado Territory, 1870; R. G. Dun and Company, "Credit Ratings for Colorado Territory," entries for Chase dated November 2, 1868; November 14, 1873; and February 16, 1874, Baker Business Library, Harvard University, Cambridge, Mass.; Forbes Parkhill, *The Wildest of the West* (New York: Henry Holt and Co., 1951), p. 66.

17. *Why,* August 23, 1890, p. 5.

18. Chase, "The Sporting Side of Denver," pp. 6, 8.

19. *Ibid.,* p. 8.

20. King, *Government of Denver,* p. 59.

21. *Rocky Mountain News,* January 13, 1889.

22. Ibid., April 2, 6, 10, 1861; Smiley, *History of Denver,* p. 428.

23. Robert E. Smith, "Thomas M. Patterson, Colorado Statehood, and the Presidential Election of 1876," *Colorado Magazine* 53 (Spring 1976): 161; Sewall Thomas, *Silhouettes of Charles S. Thomas: Colorado Governor and United States Senator* (Caldwell, Idaho: Caxton Printers, 1959), p. 21.

Chapter 5

1. Mark Twain, *Roughing It* (Hartford, Conn.: American Publishing Co., 1872), pp. 339–40.

2. *Denver City Directory* (1873), p. 32.

3. In this book a saloonkeeper is defined as any person who owns a business where alcoholic beverages are sold for consumption on the premises and is distinguished from a bartender or barkeeper working for a saloonkeeper.

4. Ray Allen Billington, in *America's Frontier Heritage* (Hinsdale, Ill.: Dryden Press, 1966), p. 221, asserts that "the key feature" of the frontier environment "was the degree of opportunity offered for upward economic and social mobility." Merle

Curti's *The Making of an American Community* (Palo Alto, Calif.: Stanford University Press, 1959) is perhaps the most notable attempt to quantify frontier mobility to date. Other quantitative studies are listed in the bibliographical notes of Billington's *Westward Expansion: A History of the American Frontier* (New York: Macmillan Co., 1966, and subsequent editions), and in Stephen Thernstrom, *The Other Bostonians: Poverty and Progress in the American Metropolis, 1880–1970* (Cambridge, Mass.: Harvard University Press, 1974), pp. 244–45.

5. In making the sometimes arbitrary distinction between blue- and white-collar workers, the "Socio-Economic Ranking of Occupations" worked out by Stephan Thernstrom in *The Other Bostonians,* app. B, pp. 289–302, has been used.

6. West, in *The Saloon on the Rocky Mountain Mining Frontier,* found that most of the poorer, blue-collar types to enter Leadville's saloon business between 1878 and 1890 "either failed miserably" or left town within a year or two. Whereas West found only 30 percent of the Leadville contingent appearing in two or more annual city directories, about 55 percent of Denver's 1858–85 operators could be found in two or more issues of the Denver directory. The higher success and persistence rate for Denver may be traced to its more stable economy.

7. R. G. Dun and Co., "Credit Ratings for Colorado Territory, entry for Florian Spalti, March 18, 1875; Frank Hall, *History of the State of Colorado,* vol. 4 (Chicago: Blakely Printing Co., 1895), p. 589.

8. Libeus Barney, *Letters,* p. 41; Libeus Barney Papers.

9. *Denver Times,* December 13, 1899.

10. Interviews with Henry H. Zietz, Jr., at the Buckhorn Exchange, Denver, February 28 and March 1, 1973.

11. Olga Curtis, "Where Denver History Rests," *Denver Post Empire Magazine,* November 22, 1970, pp. 60–65.

12. "Denver Death Index, A-7," Colorado Health Department, Bureau of Vital Statistics, Denver.

13. *Rocky Mountain News,* December 5, 1872.

14. Ibid., March 14, 1875.

15. Internal Revenue Act of July 1, 1862 (12 Stat. 432) and the U.S. Internal Revenue Assessment List for the Territory of Colorado, 1862–1873, National Archives Microfilm Publications, microcopy no. 757, Federal Records Center, Denver.

16. *Rocky Mountain News,* March 3, 1873.

17. The Depressions of 1873 and 1893 may have caused greater job turnover. However, the considerably lower mobility rates for the 1893–94 depression years (which hit Denver much harder than the 1873 Panic) suggest that mobility was indeed declining regardless of the depression cycle.

18. Compare these findings with Stephan Thernstrom's conclusions in his *The Other Bostonians,* p. 224, that "over the span of a century and two-thirds [1880–1970], there was no clear long-term trend toward either increased or decreased population mobility in the United States."

Chapter 6

1. See table 1, "Foreign Born Population of Denver, 1860–1890," compiled

from federal census data, in Stephen J. Leonard, "The Irish, English, and Germans in Denver, 1860–1890," *Colorado Magazine* 54 (Spring 1977): 129.

2. *Souvenir des Denver Turnveriens* (Denver, 1890), p. 9; Frank S. Woodbury, *Tourists' Guide to Denver* (Denver: Times Steam Printing House and Blank Book Manufacturing, 1882), p. 58; Jake Schaetzel, *Memories of Denver: Story of His Boyhood When Denver was Young and Wild, 1887 . . . 1965* (Denver: privately printed, 1970), pp. 57–64, 82; Vickers, *City of Denver,* p. 291.

3. Stephen J. Leonard, "Denver's Foreign Born Immigrants," p. 110.

4. "Letters of Frederick Steinhauer," translated from German by Karl Steinhauer, *Colorado Magazine* 10 (July 1933): 156–58.

5. This account of the orchestrion is drawn from Sanford A. Linscome, "A History of Musical Development in Denver, Colorado, 1858–1908" (Ph.D. diss., University of Texas, Austin, 1970), pp. 65–66.

6. *Denver Post,* February 2, 1899.

7. Lyle W. Dorsett, "The Ordeal of Colorado's Germans During World War I," *Colorado Magazine* 51 (Fall 1974).

8. *Rocky Mountain News,* July 14, 1865.

9. Ibid., November 11, 1881.

10. Interview with Dennis Gallagher and Cortland Doyle, Denver, January 12, 1978; *Denver Post,* December 9, 1941.

11. Interview with Thomas Flaherty, Denver, December 31, 1974.

12. "Voters' League Materials," Edward Costigan Papers, Western Historical Collections, Norlin Library, University of Colorado, Boulder.

13. *Rocky Mountain News,* March 11, 1889.

14. Marjorie Hornbein, *Temple Emanuel of Denver: A Centennial History* (Denver: Temple Emanuel, 1974), pp. 14–16.

15. Dun and Co., *"Credit Ratings,"* entries for Samuel Rose dated November 14, 1871, and November 2, 1874, Baker Business Library, Harvard University, Cambridge, Mass.

16. William M. Kramer, ed., "The Western Journal of Isaac Mayer Wise," *Western States Jewish Historical Quarterly* 5 (January 1973): 122–23.

17. Ida L. Uchill, *Pioneers, Peddlars and Tsadikim* (Denver: Sage Books, 1957), pp. 156–58.

18. Dun and Co., "Credit Ratings," entries for Angelo and Mary Ann Capelli, September 5, 1873, and August 13, 1875; Giovanni Perilli, *Colorado and the Italians in Colorado* (Denver: Smith-Brooks Press, 1922), pp. 27, 159.

19. Interview with Louis Albi, Denver, February 7, 1975.

20. David J. Cook, *Hands Up; or, Twenty Years of Detective Life in the Mountains and on the Plains* (Norman: University of Oklahoma Press, 1958), pp. 12–37; G. N. Scamehorn, *Behind the Scenes; or Denver by Gas Light* (Denver: Geo. A. Shirley Pub., 1894), p. 59; Christine A. DeRose, "Inside 'Little Italy': Italian Immigrants in Denver," *Colorado Magazine* 54 (Summer 1977): 277–93.

21. Interview with Addah Mangini Joy, Denver, March 9, 1979; *Denver Post Zone 3 Supplement,* May 19, 1976.

22. *Denver Times,* March 17, 1901.

23. Colvin G. Goddykoontz, "The People of Colorado," in LeRoy R. Hafen, ed., *Colorado and Its People,* 4 vols. (New York: Lewis Historical Publishing Co., 1948), 2:83.

24. Interview with Frank Makowski, Denver, April 21, 1977.

25. Senate Document no. 122, *A Report on Labor Disturbances in the State of Colorado, from 1880 to 1904, Inclusive,* 58th Cong., 3rd Sess., p. 133.

26. Interview with Joseph Tekavec, Denver, February 22, 1977, and interview with Jim Wright, Denver, June 7, 1981.

27. M. James Kedro, "Czecks and Slovaks in Colorado, 1860–1920," *Colorado Magazine* 54 (Spring 1977): 110.

28. John M. Barker, *The Saloon Problem and Social Reform* (Boston: Everett Press, 905), p. 11.

29. *Denver Times,* May 17, 1887.

30. Interview with John Popovich, Denver, October 20, 1977.

31. *The Saloon Problem,* Barker, p. 49. In his definitive study, "Dry Crusade: The Prohibition Movement in Colorado," Elliott West concludes: "Wets and drys differed not in whether they lived in city or country—they could be found in both places—nor in their occupations or economic positions but in their religion, ethnic background and cultural makeup" (pp. 389–90). Joseph R. Gusfield, in *Symbolic Crusade: Status Politics and the American Temperance Movement* (Urbana: University of Illinois, 1963), reaches a similar conclusion.

32. Kenneth T. Jackson, *The Ku Klux Klan in the City, 1915–1930* (New York: Oxford University Press, 1967), pp. 215–31; and Robert A. Goldberg, "Hooded Empire: The Ku Klux Klan in Colorado, 1921–1932" Ph.D. diss., University of Wisconsin, 1977.

33. *Denver Post,* January 1, 1916.

Chapter 7

1. U.S. Census Bureau, *Eleventh Census, 1890,* 4, pt. 2, "Vital Statistics of Cities of 100,000 Inhabitants and Upward for the Census Year Ending May 31, 1890" (Washington: Government Printing Office, 1893), pp. 3–4. Arthur M. Schlesinger, Sr., Richard Wade, Duane A. Smith, and, most recently, John W. Reps, in his *Cities of the American West: A History of Frontier Urban Planning* (Princeton: Princeton University Press, 979), have all emphasized the impact of the urban frontier on the American West, that western cities were modeled on eastern ones and often had more in common with the urban East than the frontier West.

2. Julian Ralph, "Colorado and Its Capital," *Harper's New Monthly Magazine* 86 (May 1893): 939.

3. I have borrowed the term *moral geography* and insight into this topic from Perry Duis, "The Saloon and the Public City: Chicago and Boston, 1880–1920" (Ph.D. diss., University of Chicago, 1975). In his extensive treatment of suburbs and saloons ("Keeping Evanston Pure," pp. 823–40), Duis argues that moral geography was rooted in a long tradition of internal districting, increasing attempts to escape the city only to have urban nuisances follow those moving to suburbs, and the neighborhood vigilante tradition.

4. *Rocky Mountain News,* January 21, 1882.

5. Ibid., December 21, 1889.

6. Ibid., February 3, 1882; February 7, 1891; and April 2, 1884.

7. Ibid., January 20, 1889; December 21, 1889; and August 29, 1890.

8. *Town of Highlands: Its Progress, Prospects and Financial Condition: First Annual Report, April, 1891* (Highlands, Colo.: Highland Chief Press, 1891), passim; Raymond Calkins, *Substitutes for the Saloon: An Investigation originally Made for the Committee of Fifty,* 2nd ed., rev. (Boston: Houghton Mifflin Co., 1919), pp. 117–18. For the history of Highlands, see Ruth E. Wiberg, *Rediscovering Northwest Denver* (Boulder, Colo.: Pruett Publishing Co., 1976).

9. Wiberg, *Rediscovering Northwest Denver,* p. 174.

10. Quoted material in this and following paragraph is from *The Road to Downington: Denver's Most Beautiful Residence Section* (Denver: Carson-Harper [1907]). Copy in author's possession courtesy of Richard Downing, Jr.

11. Ibid.

12. *Montclair, Colorado: The Beautiful Suburban Town of Denver, Colo., U.S.A.* (Denver: C. J. Kelly, 1885); *Montclair Mirror,* September 26, 1903; *Rocky Mountain News,* May 8, 1889; *Ordinances of the Town of Montclair Passed by the Board of Trustees* (Denver: Coleman and Norvell, 1891), p. 36.

13. *Denver Eye,* January 1, 1890.

14. U.S.Census Bureau, *Eleventh Census, 1890,* 4, pt. 2, pp. 3–4.

15. *Rocky Mountain News,* April 7, 1890.

16. Town of Valverde vs. Shattuck, 19 Colo. 104, pp. 104–22.

Chapter 8

1. *Denver Post,* November 19, 1912; *Rocky Mountain News,* September 28, 1897. For a study of how breweries sought a national market, see Thomas C. Cochran, *The Pabst Brewing Company* (New York: New York University Press, 1948).

2. *Rocky Mountain News,* March 28, 1892.

3. Dun and Co. "Credit Ratings," entries for Adolph Coors, dated September 27, 1873, and May 2, 1874.

4. Benjamin M. Hurwitz Papers, Western History Department, Denver Public Library.

5. Ibid. Letter from Executive Board of Denver Saloonkeepers' Union No. 1 to Denver Commissioner of Safety, Alexander Nesbit, August 6, 1914.

6. Hurwitz Papers; Louis H. Blonger, Case 403, April 7, 1900, Louis Klipfel, Case 565, April 22, 1901, and other cases in Bankruptcy Docket No. 2, Record Group 21, "Records of the U.S. District Courts, District of Colorado," Federal Records Center, Denver.

7. *Rocky Mountain News,* December 21, 1889; "Investigation of Denver Fire and Police Board Concerning Charges of Vice and Corruption, 1903," Governor James H. Peabody Papers, Colorado State Archives, Denver. Practically all the disciplinary letters sent to saloons between 1911 and 1916 by the Denver Fire and Police Board went to bars owned by· breweries or saloons whose licenses were owned by breweries. See Denver Fire and Police Board Correspondence, 1911–16, Denver Police Department.

8. Peabody Papers.

9. The Keeley Institute ran ads in Denver's daily newspapers and other early twentieth-century popular publications; *Denver Republican,* April 13, 1897; *Bien-*

nial Report of the Colorado Insane Asylum 1903–04 (Denver: Smith-Brooks Printing Co., 1905), p. 10; annual crime statistics in Sam Howe Scrapbooks, State Historical Society of Colorado Library, Denver.

10. John S. Billings, *A Summary of Investigations Conducted by the Committee of Fifty, 1893–1903* (Boston: Houghton Mifflin Co., 1905), p. 133; James H. Timberlake, *Prohibition and the Progressive Movement* (Cambridge, Mass.: Harvard University Press, 1966), p. 71.

11. Timberlake, *Prohibition,* p. 98; John D. Fitzgerald, "An Up-To-Date Horseshoeing Establishment," *International Horseshoer's Magazine* 8 (June 1907); 20.

12. *Pacific Wine, Brewing and Spirit Review* 56 (February 1914); 47.

13. Senate Document no. 122, *A Report on Labor Disturbances in the State of Colorado, From 1880 to 1904, Inclusive,* 58th Cong., 3d Sess., p. 133; *Denver Republican,* July 4, 1903. For a managerial view of the strike, see James E. Fell, Jr., *Ores to Metals: The Rocky Mountain Smelting Industry* (Lincoln: University of Nebraska Press, 1979).

14. *Denver Republican,* July 4, 1903.

15. *Laws Passed at the Ninth Session of the General Assembly of the State of Colorado* (Denver: Collier and Cleveland Lithographing Co., 1891), p. 315.

16. Peabody Papers.

17. Parkhill, *Wildest of the West,* p. 22. See also the Peabody Papers for a 1902 eyewitness account of Market Street activities.

18. Ben B. Lindsey and Harvey J. O'Higgins, *The Beast* (New York: Doubleday, Page and Co., 1910), pp. 97–99.

19. Marjorie Hornbein, "Josephine Roche: Social Worker and Coal Operator," *Colorado Magazine* 53 (Summer 1976): 243–60.

20. *Rocky Mountain News,* March 30, 1880; *Denver Medical Times,* no. 22 (1903), p. 392; Henry O. Whiteside, "The Drug Habit in Nineteenth-century Colorado," *Colorado Magazine* 55 (Winter 1978): 47–68.

21. Denver Juvenile Court, *The Problem of the Children and How the State of Colorado Cares for Them* (Denver, 1904), p. 55; Lindsey and O'Higgins, *The Beast,* p. 328.

22. Undated newspaper clipping in the Sam Howe Scrapbooks, I (1885), see also Thomas J. Noel, "Gay Bars and the Emergence of the Denver Homosexual Community," *Social Science Journal* 15 (April 1978): 59–74.

23. *Rocky Mountain News,* February 7, 1891; May 29, 1889; and January 22, 1891.

24. Inez Hunt and Wanetta W. Draper, *To Colorado's Restless Ghosts* (Denver: Sage Books, 1960), pp. 34–40.

25. *Rocky Mountain News,* November 30, 1884.

26. Cook, Hands Up, pp. 7–8. The Sam Howe Scrapbooks of the Colorado Historical Society document numerous other fencing operations.

27. Jon M. Kingsdale, in "The 'Poor Man's Club': Social Functions of the Urban Working-Class Saloon," *American Quarterly* 25 (October 1973); 472–89 found the major functions of the saloon to be a neighborhood social center, a transmitter of male culture, and a transmitter of working-class and immigrant culture. For a contemporary study of the same subject, see E. E. LeMasters, *Blue-Collar*

Aristocrats: Life-Styles at a Working-Class Tavern (Madison: University of Wisconsin Press, 1975).

28. *Denver Times,* January 6, 1887.

29. Descriptions in the following two paragraphs of the Bismarck, Watrous, Stauffer's, and the Wayside are all from the *Rocky Mountain News,* April 23, 1909.

Chapter 9

1. *Why Magazine,* April 19, 1890, p. 4; R. G. Dill, *The Political Campaigns of Colorado* (Denver: Arapahoe Publishing Co., 1895), pp. 70–75; David Day's satirical criticism in his Ouray newspaper, *The Solid Muldoon,* and elsewhere has been widely reprinted; James "Fitz-Mac" McCarthy, *Political Portraits* (Colorado Springs: Gazette Publishing Co., 1888), pp. 209–10.

2. *Rocky Mountain News,* November 23, 1882.

3. Cited in Elliott West, "Dirty Tricks in Denver," *Colorado Magazine* 52 (Summer 1975): 236. West's article details and documents the election fraud and subsequent trial.

4. *Rocky Mountain News,* March 21, 1889.

5. Ibid., April 2, 1889.

6. West, "Dirty Tricks in Denver," p. 236.

7. *Rocky Mountain News,* April 3, 1889; *Denver Republican,* November 28, 1889.

8. *Rocky Mountain News,* March 31, 1890.

9. Ibid., August 4, 1889.

10. *Harper's Weekly,* April 8, 1893. December 16, 1891, p. 27.

11. *Laws Passed at the Seventh Session,* p. 126; *Charter of the City of Denver* (Denver: F. W. Robinson, 1893), p. 13; King, *Government of Denver,* pp. 184–85.

12. Elliott West, "Dry Crusade: The Prohibition Movement in Colorado," p. 200.

13. *Rocky Mountain News,* October 4, 1897.

14. "Voters' League report on the 1905–6 Denver city council meetings and assessment of John Conlon at March 3, 1906, meeting," Costigan Papers.

15. "The System," Costigan Papers.

16. *Voters' Bulletin* 1 (April 1906); 2–3.

17. "Voters' League Assessment of John P. Jones, March 13, 1906," Costigan Papers; *Voters' Bulletin* 1 (April 1906); 3.

18. "Extract from Proceedings of a Meeting of the Board of Aldermen held on Monday Evening, November 13, 1906," and "Voters' League Assessment of City Councilmen, 1906," Costigan Papers; *Voters' Bulletin* 1 (April 1906): 3.

19. Ibid.; see also obituaries for Conlon in the *Denver Post,* December 6, 1922, and *Rocky Mountain News,* December 7, 1922.

20. "Voters' League Assessment of City Councilmen, 1906," Costigan Papers.

21. *Municipal Facts,* April 24, 1909, p. 14.

22. "Report on City Councilmen, 1906," Costigan Papers.

23. Frank E. Rider, "The Denver Police Department: An Administrative, Organizational and Occupational History" (Ph.D. diss., University of Denver, 1971), p.

491. See also John R. Pickering, "Blueprint of Power: Robert Speer's Years in Denver" (Ph.D. diss., University of Denver, 1978).

24. *Denver Times,* May 10, 1904; Benjamin Lindsey and Harvey J. O'Higgins, *The Beast* (New York: Doubleday and Co., 1910), p. 184.

25. *Denver Republican,* October 22, 1902; Edward Keating, *The Gentleman from Colorado* (Denver: Sage Books, 1964), p. 197.

26. Charles A. Johnson, *Denver's Mayor Speer* (Denver: Green Mountain Press, 1969), pp. 1–2, 4–5.

27. *Revised Municipal Code of the City and County of Denver* (Denver, 1906), p. 709.

28. Lindsey and O'Higgins, *The Beast,* pp. 59–62.

29. Ibid., p. 204.

30. Ibid., p. 184.

31. *Denver Post,* July 3, 1901; Lindsey and O'Higgins, *The Beast,* pp. 89, 90–91; 29 Colo. 448; 192 U.S. 108.

32. Case 2088, September 30, 1912, Criminal Docket Book No. 31, Denver District Court.

33. George W. Creel, *Rebel at Large: Recollections of a Crowded Fifty Years* (New York: Putnam and Sons, 1947), p. 104.

34. "Denver Fire and Police Board Correspondence," Letter of February 13, 1913, Denver Police Department Library.

35. "Unpublished Memoirs of Governor Charles S. Thomas," p. 145, Charles S. Thomas Papers, State Historical Society of Colorado, Denver; official election returns for city election, September 12, 1916, Denver Election Commission.

36. Johnson, *Denver's Mayor Speer,* p. 1.

37. *Rocky Mountain News* and *Denver Post,* September 28, 1921; *Trail* 4 (October 1921); 5; interview with Arthur Bowdim, Ed Chase's chauffeur, February 3, 1967, State Historical Society of Colorado, Denver.

38. Parkhill, *Wildest of the West,* pp. 80–84; Keating, *Gentleman from Colorado,* pp. 311–12; "Last Will and Testament of Vaso L. Chucovich," Denver Probate Court, case 52705.

Chapter 10

1. Robert L. Brown, "Saloons of the American West," *Denver Westerners Roundup* 29 (March-April 1973): 3–19.

2. Rachel Wild Peterson, *The Long Lost Rachel Wild or, Seeking Diamonds in the Rough: Her Life in the Slums of Denver* (Denver: Reed Publishing Co., 1905), pp. 257–58; George N. Rainsford, "Dean Henry Martyn Hart and Public Issues," *Colorado Magazine* 48 (Summer 1971): 210–11.

3. Quoted in Alfred M. Lee, "Techniques of Social Reform: An Analysis of the New Prohibition Drive," *American Sociological Review,* no. 9 (1944), pp. 65–77.

4. *Union Signal,* July 4, 1907; the poem is quoted in West, "Dry Crusade: The Prohibition Movement in Colorado," p. 138.

5. John M. Barker, *The Saloon Problem and Social Reform* (Boston: Everett Press, 1905), p. 193.

6. Letter of Rev. Edwin E. McLaughlin, State Superintendent of the Anti-

Saloon League of Colorado, to his coworkers, January 25, 1911, Benjamin M. Hurwitz Papers, Western History Department, Denver Public Library.

7. "Liquor Code of 1935," *Session Laws of Colorado* (Denver: Eames Brothers, 1935), p. 597.

8. U.S. Department of Commerce, Bureau of the Census, *General Statistics of the Cities: 1915* (Washington: Government Printing Office, 1915).

BIBLIOGRAPHY

Archival Sources

Berkeley. University of California. Bancroft Library. Great Britain. Board of Trade. Registrar of Companies Office. Papers of Denver United Breweries, Ltd. Microfilm copy.

————.————.————. "By ox team to California: a narrative of crossing the plains in 1860" [by Lavinia (Honeyman) Porter].

Boulder. University of Colorado. Norlin Library. Western Historical Collection. Edward P. Costigan Papers.

Cambridge, Mass. Harvard University. Baker Business Library. "Credit Ratings for Colorado Territory" [by R. G. Dun and Company].

Denver. Colorado State Archives. Governors' Papers. James Peabody Papers.

————. Public Library. Western History Dept. Reverend A. T. Rankin Diary.

————.————.————. Benjamin Hurwitz papers.

————. State Historical Society of Colorado. Libeus Barney papers.

————.————. Candelight Club Minutes.

————.————. Edward Chase, "The Sporting Side of Denver," an interview conducted by Thomas F. Dawson.

————.————. Sam Howe Scrapbooks.

————.————. "Map of the City of Denver Showing Cable and Steam Railways, January 28, 1893."

————.————. Charles S. Thomas Papers.

————.————. Manuscript biography. Baron Eugene A. von Winckler.

San Marino, Calif. Huntington Library. Levien Collection.

Government Publications

Federal

U.S. Department of Commerce. Bureau of the Census. *General Statistics of the Cities: 1915.* Washington: Government Printing office, 1915.

————. Manuscript Censuses of 1860, 1870, 1880, and 1900 for Denver City, Arapahoe County, Colorado. Microfilm. Federal Record Center, Denver.

————. *Population of the United States in 1860.* Washington: Government Printing Office, 1864.

133

————. *Population of the United States, Ninth Census.* Washington: Government Printing Office, 1872.

————. *Population of the United States in 1880, Tenth Census.* Washington: Government Printing Office, 1883.

————. *Eleventh Census, 1890.* Washington: Government Printing Office, 1893.

U.S. Congress. Senate. *A Report on Labor Disturbances in the State of Colorado, from 1880 to 1904, Inclusive. Senate Document* no. 122, 58th Cong. 3rd sess.

U.S. District Court for Colorado. Civil Case Files, 1880. Case 483. *Richard E. Whitsitt vs. Union Depot Railroad Company et al.*

————. *Denver Bankruptcy Case File.* Federal Records Center, Denver.

U.S. Geological Survey. *Historic Trail Map of the Greater Denver Area, Colorado.* Washington: USGS Miscellaneous Information Series, 1976.

U.S. Internal Revenue Assessment List for the Territory of Colorado, 1862–73. National Archives Microfilm Publications. Federal Records Center, Denver.

State

Biennial Report of the Colorado Insane Asylum, 1903–04. Denver: Smith-Brooks Printing Co., 1905.

Death Records, Bureau of Vital Statistics, Colorado Health Department, Denver.

Laws Passed at the First Session of the General Assembly of the State of Colorado. Denver, 1877.

Laws Passed at the Seventh Session of the General Assembly of the State of Colorado. Denver: Collier and Cleveland Lithographing Co., 1889.

Laws Passed at the Ninth Session of the General Assembly of the State of Colorado. Denver: Smith-Brooks Printing Co., 1893.

Laws Passed at the Thirtieth Session of the General Assembly of the State of Colorado. Denver: Eames Brothers, 1935.

Session Laws of Colorado Territory. Central City: David C. Collier, 1866.

Municipal

Charter of the City and County of Denver. Denver: Publishers Press Room and Bindery Co., 1904.

Charter of the City of Denver. Denver: F. W. Robinson, 1893.

The Charter and Ordinances of the City of Denver. Denver, 1862.

The Charter and Ordinances of the City of Denver. Denver: Byers and Dailey, 1866.

The Charter and Ordinances of the City of Denver. Denver: Denver Publishing House, 1878.

The City Charter of Denver. Denver: News Printing Co., 1862.

Compiled Ordinances and Charter: The City of Denver. Compiled by Henry T. Hershy. Denver: Smith-Brooks Printing Co., 1898.

Denver Election Commission. Voting returns.

Denver Fire and Police Board. Correspondence. Denver Police Dept. Library

Denver Fire and Police Departments Illustrated. Denver: Smith-Brooks Printing Co., 1905.

Denver Juvenile Court. *The Problem of the Children and How the State of Colorado Cares for Them.* Denver, 1904.

Bibliography

Denver Municipal Facts. Denver: City and county of Denver, 1909–31.
Denver Revised Municipal Code, 1881. Denver: 1881.
Ordinances of the Town of Montclair Passed by the Board of Trustees. Denver:
    Coleman and Norvell, 1891. Western History Dept., Denver Public Library.
Revised Municipal Code of the City and County of Denver. Denver, 1906.
State Historical Society of Colorado. "Proceedings of the Denver City Council."

Newspapers and Periodicals

Cervi's Rocky Mountain Journal (Denver)
Colorado Magazine (Denver)
Colorado Tribune (Denver)
Denver Daily Gazette
Denver Daily News
Denver Daily Times
Denver Express
Denver Eye
Denver Medical Times
Denver Post
Denver Republican
Denver Times
Denver Tribune
Denver Westerners Roundup
Frank Leslie's Illustrated Newspaper (New York)
Inter-Ocean: A Journal of Colorado Politics, Society, and Mining (Denver)
Jewish Outlook
Mida's Criterion (Chicago)
Montclair Mirror (Montclair, Colo.).
Pacific Historical Review
Pacific Wine, Brewing and Spirit Review (San Francisco)
Rocky Mountain Presbyterian (Denver)
Rocky Mountain News (Denver)
Smithsonian Magazine
Solid Muldoon (Ouray, Colo.)
Union Signal WCTU (Evanston, Ill.)
Voters' Bulletin (Denver)
Western Mountaineer (Golden, Colo.)
Why Magazine (Denver)

Legal Citations

Federal

Crowley v. Christiansen (137 U.S. 86).
192 U.S. 108.

State

Schwartz v. People (46 Colorado 239).
29 Colorado 448. *Town of Valverde vs. Shattuck* (19 Colorado 104).

Municipal

Denver District Court. Criminal Court. Docket Book No. 31. Case 2088, September 30, 1912.

Denver Probate Court. Case 52705. Last Will and Testament of Vaso L. Chucovich.

Books and Pamphlets

Adolph Coors Company. *The Pre-prohibition History of Adolph Coors Company, 1873–1933.* Denver, 1973.

Ade, George. *The Old Time Saloon.* New York: R. Long and R. R. Smith, 1931.

A Reliable Directory of the Pleasure Resorts of Denver. Denver [?], 1892.

Arps, Louisa Ward. *Denver in Slices.* Denver: Sage Books, 1959.

———. *Faith on the Frontier.* Denver: Colorado Council of Churches, 1976

Athearn, Robert G. *Westward the Briton.* New York: Charles Scribner's Sons, 1953.

———. *Rebel of the Rockies: The Denver and Rio Grande Western Railroad.* New Haven: Yale University Press, 1962.

———. *Union Pacific Country.* Chicago: Rand McNally and Co., 1971.

———. *The Coloradans.* Albuquerque: University of New Mexico Press, 1977.

Atherton, Lewis. *Main Street on the Middle Border.* Bloomington: University of Indiana Press, 1954.

Bancroft, Caroline. *Six Racy Madams of Colorado.* Boulder, Colo.: Johnson Publishing Co., 1965.

Barker, John M. *The Saloon Problem and Social Reform.* Boston: Everett Press, 1905.

Barney, Libeus. *Letters of the Pike's Peak Gold Rush.* San Jose, Calif.: Talisman Press, 1959.

Baron, Stanley. *Brewed in America: A History of Beer and Ale in the United States.* Boston: Little, Brown and Co., 1962.

Barrett, William E. "The Man from Rome," in *Denver Murders,* edited by Lee Casey. New York: Duell, Sloan and Pearce, 1946.

Betz, Larry. *Globeville: Part of Colorado's History.* Denver: privately printed, 1972.

Billings, John S., et al. *The Liquor Problem: A Summary of Investigations Conducted by the Committee of Fifty, 1893–1903.* Boston: Houghton Mifflin Co., 1905.

Billington, Ray Allen. *Westward Expansion: A History of the American Frontier.* New York: Macmillan, 1966.

———. *America's Frontier Heritage.* Hinsdale. Ill.: Dryden Press, 1966.

Bird, Isabella. *A Lady's Life in the Rocky Mountains.* Norman: University of Oklahoma Press, 1960.

Birge, Julius C. *The Awakening of the Desert.* Boston: Gorham Press, 1912.

Boorstin, Daniel J. *The Americans: The National Experience.* New York: Random House, 1965.

Boyer, Richard O., and Morais, Herbert M. *Labor's Untold Story.* New York: United Electrical, Radio and Machine Workers of America, 1955.

Breck, Allen D. *The Centennial History of the Jews of Colorado.* Denver: University of Denver, 1960.

———. *William Gray Evans: Portrait of a Western Executive.* Denver: University of Denver, 1964.

Bibliography

Brown, Robert L. *Saloons of the American West.* Silverton, Colo.: Sundance Books, 1978.

Calkins, Raymond. *Substitutes for the Saloon: An Investigation Originally Made for the Committee of Fifty.* 2d ed., rev. Boston: Houghton Mifflin Company, 1919.

Caven, Sherri. *Liquor License: An Ethnography of Bar Behavior.* Chicago: Aldine Press, 1966.

Clint, David K. and Company, compilers. *Colorado Historical Bottles and Etc.* Denver: Antique Bottle Collectors of Colorado, 1976.

Cochran, Thomas C. *The Pabst Brewing Company.* New York: New York University Press, 1948.

Colorado Telephone Company. *The Colorado Telephone Company List of Subscribers.* Denver: 1880.

Conard, Howard Louis. *Uncle Dick Wootton: The Pioneer Frontiersman of the Rocky Mountain Region.* Chicago: R. R. Donnelley and Sons, 1957.

Conoco: The First One Hundred Years. New York: Dell Publishing Co., 1975.

Cook, Davis J. *Hands Up; or, Twenty Years of Detective Life in the Mountains and on the Plains.* Norman: University of Oklahoma Press, 1958.

Creel, George W. *Rebel at Large: Recollections of a Crowded Fifty Years.* New York: Putnam and Sons, 1947.

Curti, Merle. *The Making of an American Community.* Palo Alto, Calif.: Stanford University Press, 1959.

Dallas, Sandra. *Gold and Gothic.* Denver: Lick Skillet Press, 1967.

————. *Cherry Creek Gothic: Victorian Architecture in Denver.* Norman: University of Oklahoma Press, 1971.

Denver City Directories.

Denver Householders' Directories. .

Dill, Robert Gorden. *Political Campaigns of Colorado, with Complete Tabulated Statements of the Official Vote.* Denver: Arapahoe Publishing Co., 1895.

Dorsett, Lyle W. *The Queen City: A History of Denver.* Boulder, Colo.: Pruett Publishing Co., 1977.

Dugal, Louis. *Explanation to Diagram of Denver, Colorado: Embracing A Small Map Showing Denver and Additions.* New York: Wynkoop and Hollenbeck, 1868.

Dykstra, Robert R. *The Cattle Towns.* New York: Alfred A. Knopf, 1968.

Erdoes, Richard. *Saloons of the Old West.* New York: Alfred A. Knopf, 1979.

Fell, James E., Jr. *Ores to Metals: The Rocky Mountain Smelting Industry.* Lincoln: University of Nebraska Press, 1979.

Flexner, Eleanor. *Century of Struggle: The Woman's Rights Movement in the United States.* Cambridge, Mass.: Harvard University Press, 1959.

Fowler, Gene. *Timberline: A Story of Bonfils and Tammen.* New York: Covici-Fried, 1933.

Fritz, Percy E. *Colorado: The Centennial State.* New York: Prentice-Hall, 1941.

Furnas, J. C. *The Life and Times of the Late Demon Rum.* New York: G. P. Putnam's Sons, 1965.

Gandolfo, Marcello. *Gil Italiani Nel Colorado.* Denver: Dove Tipographo, n.d.

Greeley, Horace. *An Overland Journey.* Edited by Charles T. Duncan. New York: Alfred A. Knopf, 1964.

Gregg, Kate L. *The Road to Santa Fe.* Albuquerque: University of New Mexico Press, 1952.

Bibliography

Gusfield, Joseph R. *Symbolic Crusade: Status Politics and the American Temperance Movement*. Urbana: University of Illinois Press, 1963.

Hafen, LeRoy R., ed. *Colorado and Its People*. 4 vols. New York: Lewis Historical Publishing Co., 1948.

Hafen, LeRoy R. and Hafen, Ann R., eds. *Reports from Colorado: The Wildman Letters, 1858–1865*. Glendale, Calif.: Arthur H. Clark Co., 1961.

Halaas, David F. *Fairmount and Historic Colorado*. Denver: Fairmount Cemetery Association, 1976.

Hall, Frank. *History of the State of Colorado*. 4 vols. Chicago: Blakely Printing Co., 1895.

Haywood, William D. *The Autobiography of William D. Haywood*. New York: International Publishers, 1929.

Hill, Alice Polk. *Colorado Pioneers in Picture and Story*. Denver: Brock-Haffner Press, 1915.

Hill, Alice Polk. *Tales of the Colorado Pioneers*. Denver: Pierson and Gardner, 1884.

Horan, J. D., and Sonn, Paul. *Pictorial History of the Wild West*. New York: Crown Publishing Co., 1954.

Hornbein, Marjorie. *Temple Emanuel of Denver: A Centennial History*. Denver: Temple Emanuel, 1974.

Hosokawa, Bill. *Thunder in the Rockies: The Incredible Denver Post*. New York: William Morrow and Co., 1976.

Hunt, Inez, and Draper, Wanetta W. *To Colorado's Restless Ghosts*. Denver: Sage Books, 1960.

Hyde, George E. *Life of George Bent, Written from His Letters*. Norman: University of Oklahoma Press, 1967.

Jackson, Kenneth T. *The Ku Klux Klan in the City, 1915–1930*. New York: Oxford University Press, 1967.

James, Henry. *The American Scene*. Bloomington: Indiana University Press, 1968.

Johnson, Charles A. *Denver's Mayor Speer*. Denver: Green Mountain Press, 1969.

Johnson, Forrest H. *Denver's Old Theatre Row: The Story of Curtis Street and Its Business*. Denver: Bill Lay, LITHO, Printers, 1970.

Keating, Edward. *The Gentleman from Colorado*. Denver: Sage Books, 1964.

Kelsey, Harry E., Jr. *Frontier Capitalist: The Life of John Evans*. Denver: State Historical Society of Colorado, 1969.

King, Clyde L. *History of the Government of Denver*. Denver: Fisher Book Co., 1911.

Knights, Peter S. *The Plain People of Boston*. New York: Oxford University Press, 1971.

Larimer, William Henry Harrison. *Reminiscences of General William Larimer and of His Son, William H. H. Larimer, Two of the Founders of Denver*, compiled by Herman S. Davis. Lancaster, Pa.: New Era Printing Co., 1918.

Le Masters, E. E. *Blue-Collar Aristocrats: Life-Styles at a Working-Class Tavern*. Madison: University of Wisconsin Press, 1975.

Lindsey, Ben B. and O'Higgins, Harvey J. *The Beast*. New York: Doubleday, Page and Co., 1910.

Long, Margaret. *The Smoky Hill Trail: Following the Old Historic Pioneer Trails on the Modern Highways*. Denver: W. H. Kistler, 1943.

Bibliography

MacCarthy, James "Fitz-Mac." *Political Portraits*. Colorado Springs: Gazette Pub. Co., 1899.

Montclair, Colorado: The Beautiful Suburban Town of Denver, Colo., U.S.A. Denver: C. J. Kelly, 1885.

Noel, Thomas J. *Denver's Larimer Street: Main Street, Skid Row and Urban Renaissance*. Denver: Historic Denver, Inc., 1981.

———. *Denver: Rocky Mountain Gold*. Tulsa: Continental Heritage Press, 1980.

———. *Richthofen's Montclair: A Pioneer Denver Suburb*. Boulder: Pruett Publishing, 1978.

Parkhill, Forbes. *The Wildest of the West*. New York: Henry Holt and Co., 1951.

———. *Mister Barney Ford: A Portrait in Bistre*. Denver: Sage Books, 1963.

Peters, Bette D. *Denver's Four Mile House*. Denver: Golden Bell Press, 1980.

Perilli, Giovanni. *Colorado and the Italians in Colorado*. Denver: Smith-Brooks Press, 1922.

Perkin, Robert L. *The First Hundred Years: An Informal History of Denver and the Rocky Mountain News*. Garden City, N.Y.: Doubleday and Co., 1959.

Peterson, Rachel Wild. *The Long Lost Rachel Wild or, Seeking Diamonds in the Rough: Her Experiences in the Slums of Denver*. Denver: Reed Publishing Co., 1905.

Pittman, D. J., and Snyder, C. R., eds. *Society, Culture and Drinking Patterns*. New York: John Wiley and Sons, 1962.

Richardson, Albert D. *Beyond the Mississippi*. Hartford, Conn.: American Publishing Co., 1867. *The Road to Downington: Denver's Most Beautiful Residence Section*. Denver: Carson-Harper [1907].

Robertson, Frank G., and Harris, Beth Kay. *Soapy Smith: King of the Frontier Con Men*. New York: Hastings House, 1961.

Scamehorn, G. N. *Behind the Scenes; or, Denver by Gas Light*. Denver: Geo. A Shirley Pub., 1894.

Schaetzel, Jake. *Memories of Denver: Story of His Boyhood When Denver was Young and Wild, 1887 . . . 1965*. Denver: privately printed, 1970.

Schoberlin, Melvin. *From Candles to Footlights: A Biography of the Pike's Peak Theatre, 1859–1876*. Denver: Old West Pub. Co., 1941.

Simonin, Louis L. *The Rocky Mountain West in 1867*. Translated and annotated by Wilson O. Clough. Lincoln: University of Nebraska Press, 1966.

Smiley, Jerome C. *History of Denver*. Denver: Times-Sun Publishing Co., 1901.

Smith, Duane A. *Rocky Mountain Mining Camps: The Urban Frontier*. Bloomington: Indiana University Press, 1967.

———. *Horace Tabor: His Life and the Legend*. Boulder: Colorado Associated University Press, 1973.

Souvenir des Denver Turnverein. Denver, 1890.

Souvenir History of the Denver Fire and Police Departments. Denver: Denver Litho, 1900.

Thernstrom, Stephan. *The Other Bostonians: Poverty and Progress in the American Metropolis, 1880–1970*. Cambridge: Harvard University Press, 1973.

Thomas, Sewall. *Silhouettes of Charles S. Thomas: Colorado Governor and United States Senator*. Caxton, Idaho: Caxton Printers, 1959.

Timberlake, James H. *Prohibition and the Progressive Movement*. Cambridge, Mass.: Harvard University Press, 1966.

Bibliography

Town of Highlands: Its Progress, Prospects and Financial Condition; First Annual Report, April, 1891. Highlands, Colo.: Highland Chief Press, 1891.

Townshend, Richard B. A Tenderfoot in Colorado. London: Butler and Tanner, 1903.

Twain, Mark. Roughing It. Hartford, Conn.: American Publishing Co., 1872.

Uchill, Ida L. Pioneers, Peddlars and Tsadikim. Denver: Sage Books, 1957.

Van Orman, Richard A. A Room for the Night: Hotels of the Old West. Bloomington: Indiana University Press, 1966.

Vickers, William B. History of the City of Denver. Chicago: O. L. Baskin and Co., 1880.

Wade, Richard C. The Urban Frontier: Pioneer Life in Early Pittsburgh, Cincinnati, Lexington, Louisville, and St. Louis. Cambridge: Harvard University Press, 1959.

Wallihan, Samuel S., and Bigney, T. O., compilers, The Rocky Mountain Directory and Colorado Gazeteer for 1871. Denver: S. S. Wallihan and Co., 1870.

West, Elliott. The Saloon on the Rocky Mountain Mining Frontier. Lincoln: University of Nebraska Press, 1979.

Western Slavonic Association. Amendments and Supplements to the By-Laws of the Western Slavonic Association. Denver, 1973.

Wharton, Junius E., and Wilhelm, David O. History of the City of Denver. Denver: Byers and Dailey, 1866.

White, John. Sketches from America. London: Sampson, Low, Son and Marston, 1870.

Wiberg, Ruth E. Rediscovering Northwest Denver. Boulder, Colo.: Pruett Publishing Co., 1976.

Winther, Oscar Osburn. The Transportation Frontier: Trans-Mississippi West, 1865–1890 New York: Holt, Rinehart, and Winston, 1964.

Woodbury, Frank S. Tourist's Guide to Denver. Denver: Times Steam Printing House and Blank Book Manufactory, 1882.

Young, John D. John D. Young and the Colorado Gold Rush. Edited by Dwight L. Smith. Chicago: R. R. Donnelley and Sons, 1969.

Articles

Boyd, Louie Croft. "Katrina Wolf Murat, the Pioneer." Colorado Magazine 16 (September 1939): 180–85.

Brown, Robert L. "Saloons of the American West." Denver Westerners Roundup 29 (March-April 1973): 3–19.

Burk, Ann. "The Mining Camp Saloon as a Social Center." Red River Valley Historical Review 2 (Fall 1975): 381–92.

Carson, Gerald. "Saloon." American Heritage Magazine 14 (April 1963): 24–31.

"Civic Progress in Denver." Harper's Weekly Magazine, 8 April 1893, p. 318.

Curtis, Olga. "The Chairman is Only Half Irish." Denver Post Empire Magazine, 9 March 1975, pp. 16–19.

———. "Where Denver History Rests." Denver Post Empire Magazine 22 November 1970, pp. 60–65.

Bibliography

DeLorme, Roland L. "Turn-of-the-Century Denver: An Invitation to Reform." *Colorado Magazine* 45 (Winter 1968): 1–15.

De Rose, Christine A. "Inside 'Little Italy': Italian Immigrants in Denver." *Colorado Magazine* 54 (Summer 1977): 277–93.

Doeppers, Daniel F. "The Globeville Neighborhood in Denver." *Geographical Review* 57 (October 1967): 506–22.

Dolman, Mrs. Samuel. "Letter." *Trail* 17 (January 1925): 11–13.

Dorsett, Lyle W. "The City Boss and the Reformer: A Reappraisal." *Pacific Northwest Quarterly* 63 (October 1972): 150–54.

————. "The Ordeal of Colorado's Germans during World War I." *Colorado Magazine* 51 (Fall 1974): 277–93.

Fitzgerald, John D. "An Up-to-Date Horseshoeing Establishment." *International Horseshoers' Magazine* 8 (June 1907): 31–34.

Hays, Samuel P. "The Politics of Reform in Municipal Government in the Progressive Era." *Pacific Northwest Quarterly* 55 (October 1964): 157–69.

Hornbein, Marjorie. "Josephine Roche: Social Worker and Coal Operator." *Colorado Magazine* 53 (Summer 1976): 243–60.

Kedro, M. James. "Czechs and Slovaks in Colorado, 1860–1920. *Colorado Magazine* 54 (Spring 1977): 92–125.

Kingsdale, Jon M. "The 'Poor Man's Club': Social Functions of the Urban Working-Class Saloon." *American Quarterly* 25 (October 1973): 472–89.

Knox, Thomas W. "To Pike's Peak and Denver." *Knickerbocker Magazine* 58 (August 1861): 115–28.

Kramer, William M., ed. "The Western Journal of Isaac Mayer Wise." *Western States Jewish Historical Quarterly* 5 (January 1973): 117–34.

Lee, Alfred M. "Techniques of Social Reform: An Analysis of the New Prohibition Drive." *American Sociological Review* 9 (1944): 65–77.

Leonard, Stephen J. "The Irish, English, and Germans in Denver, 1860–1890." *Colorado Magazine* 54 (Spring 1977): 126–53.

"Letters of Frederick Steinhauer." Translated from German by Karl Steinhauer. *Colorado Magazine* 10 (July 1933): 156–58.

Low, Edith Parker. "History of the Twenty Mile House on Cherry Creek." *Colorado Magazine* 12 (July 1935): 142–44.

Mann, Ralph W. "The Decade After the Gold Rush: Social Structure in Grass Valley and Nevada City, California, 1850–1860." *Pacific Historical Review* 46 (November 1972): 484–504.

Melvin, Jane. "The Twelve Mile House." *Colorado Magazine* 12 (September 1935): 173–78.

Mitchell, J. Paul. "Boss Speer and the City Functional." *Pacific Northwest Quarterly* 63 (October 1972): 155–64.

Noel, Thomas J. "Gay Bars and the Emergence of the Denver Homosexual Community." *Social Science Journal* 15 (April 1978): 59–74.

Rainsford, George N. "Dean Henry Martyn Hart and Public Issues." *Colorado Magazine* 48 (Summer 1971): 204–20.

Ralph, Julian. "Colorado and Its Capital." *Harper's New Monthly Magazine* 86 (May 1893): 935–48.

Rogers, Platt. "Municipal Condition of Denver." National Municipal League, *Proceedings of the Third National Conference, 1894*. Philadelphia, 1895.

Smith, Joseph Emerson. "Personal Recollections of Early Denver." *Colorado Magazine* 20 (January 1943): 5–16.

Smith, Robert E. "Thomas M. Patterson, Colorado Statehood, and the Presidential Election of 1876." *Colorado Magazine* 53 (Spring 1976): 153–62.

Tank, Robert M. "Mobility and Occupational Structure on the Late Nineteenth-Centuy Urban Frontier: The Case of Denver, Colorado." *Pacific Historical Review* 47 (May 1978): 189–216.

Thomas, J. J. "In the Days of the Overland Trail." *Trail* 2 (May 1910): 5–9.

Von Schmidt, Eric. "Custer, Dying Again at that Last Stand, Is in a New Painting." *Smithsonian Magazine* 7 (June 1976): 58–65.

West, Elliott. "Cleansing the Queen City: Prohibition and Urban Reform in Denver." *Arizona and the West* 14 (Winter 1972): 331–46.

West, William Elliott. "Dirty Tricks in Denver." *Colorado Magazine* 52 (Summer 1975): 225–43.

Whiteside, Henry O. "The Drug Habit in Nineteenth-Century Colorado." *Colorado Magazine* 55 (Winter 1978): 46–68.

Working, D. W. "History of the Four Mile House." *Colorado Magazine* 18 (November 1941): 209–13.

Wortman, Roy T. "Denver's Anti-Chinese Riot, 1880." *Colorado Magazine* 42 (Fall, 1965): 275–91.

Younker, Jason T. "The Early Pioneer, Reminiscences of 1858–59." *Trail* 2 (January 1910): 5–12.

Interviews

Albi, Louis, Denver, February 7, 1975.

Arps, Louisa Ward, Denver, June 24, 1977.

Bowdim, Arthur, Denver, February 3, 1967.

Doyle, Cortland, Denver, January 12, 1978.

Flaherty, Thomas, Denver, December 31, 1974.

Gallagher, Dennis, Denver, March 17, 1977.

Gotterdam, Annette Zang, Denver, September 15, 1976.

Makowski, Frank, Denver, April 21, 1977.

Mangini, Addah Joy, Denver, March 9, 1979.

Popovich, John, Denver, October 20, 1977.

Takavec, Joseph, Denver, February 22, 1977.

Woolley, Charles, Denver, June 18, 1978.

Zietz, Henry H., Jr., Denver, February 28, March 1, 1973.

Dissertations

DeLorme, Roland. "The Shaping of a Progressive; Edward P. Costigan and Municipal Reform in Denver." Ph.D. dissertation, University of Colorado, 1965.

Duis, Perry. "The Saloon and the Public City: Chicago and Boston, 1880–1920." Ph.D. dissertation, University of Chicago, 1975.

Goldberg, Robert Alan. "Hooded Empire: The Ku Klux Klan in Colorado, 1921–1932." Ph.D. dissertation, University of Wisconsin, 1977.

Bibliography

Fuller, Leon. "The Populist Regime in Colorado." Ph.D. dissertation, University of Wisconsin, 1933.

Huber, Frances Anne. "The Progressive Career of Ben B. Lindsey, 1900–1920." Ph.D. dissertation, University of Michigan, 1963.

Kedro, James Milo. "Stanley Wood and the Great Divide." Ph.D. dissertation, University of Denver, 1976.

Leonard, Stephen J. "Denver's Foreign Born Immigrants, 1859–1900." Ph.D. dissertation, Claremont College, 1971.

Linscome, Sanford A. "A History of Musical Development in Denver, Colorado, 1858–1908." Ph.D. dissertation, University of Texas at Austin, 1970.

Pickering, John R. "Blueprint of Power: Robert Speer's Years in Denver." Ph.D. dissertation, University of Denver, 1978.

Rider, Frank E. "The Denver Police Department: An Administrative, Organizational and Occupational History." Ph.D. dissertation, University of Denver, 1971.

Rosen, Bernard. "Poverty and Social Welfare in Denver, 1858–1900." Ph.D. dissertation, University of Colorado, 1976.

Walker, Henry P. "The Rise and Decline of High Plains Freighting, 1822–1880." Ph.D. dissertation, University of Colorado, 1965.

West, William Elliott. "Dry Crusade: The Prohibition Movement in Colorado, 1858–1933." Ph.D. dissertation, University of Colorado, 1971.

Index